NORTH AMERICAN RAIL TRANSIT

1991

Washington Metro Area Transit Authority

Printed in the United States of America

Library of Congress Catalog Card Number:
91-062682

North American Rail Transit

Published by:
American Public Transit Association
1201 New York Avenue, N.W.
Washington D.C., 20005
(202) 898-4000

San Francisco Bay Area Metropolitan
Transportation Commission
MertoCenter
101 Eighth Street
Oakland, California 94607
(415) 464-7700

Santa Clara County Transit District
Board of Supervisors
70 West Hedding Street
San Jose, California 95110
(408) 299-2323

Edited by:
APTA Vice President - Rail Transit,
Rod Diridon
with Colleen Crowley and Rick Kitson

Printed by:
Jostens
Visalia, California

1991

North American Rail Transit

Contents

American Public Transit Association
Executive Board

Alan F. Kiepper
Chairman

Louis H. Parsons
Vice Chairman

Richard J. Simonetta
Secretary-Treasurer

Daniel T. Scannell
*Immediate
Past Chairman*

Jack R. Gilstrap
*Executive
Vice President*

Vice Presidents

John A. Bonsall
Canadian Members

Terry O. Cooper
Government Affairs

Rod Diridon
Rail Transit

Anthony M. Kouneski
Bus Operations

Thomas P. Kujawa
Marketing

Mark J. Obert
*Associate
Member-At-Large*

Hershel R. Payne
Governing Boards

Turner M. Spencer
Human Resources

Ronald J. Tober
*Management and
Finance*

David L. Turney
Associate Members

John L. Wilson
Small Operations

4

APTA Designated Directors

Agency	Professional	Policy Board
Chicago Transit Authority	Alfred H. Savage, *Exec. Dir.*	Clark Burrus, *Chair*
Greater Cleveland Regional Transit Authority	Ronald J. Tober, *GM, Sec.-Tres.*	Earl Martin, *Pres., Bd. of Trustees*
Mass Transit Administration of Maryland	Ronald J. Hartman, *GM, Admin.*	James Lighthizer, *Sec., MD DOT*
Massachusetts Bay Transportation Authority	James E. Rooney, *Acting GM*	Scott M. Stearns, *Bd. Member*
Metropolitan Atlanta Rapid Transit Authority	Kenneth M. Gregor, *GM*	Ryland N. McClendon, *Chair*
Metro-Dade Transit Agency	Chester E. Colby, *Dir.*	Charles Dusseau, *Chair*
Metropolitan Transportation Authority	Alan F. Kiepper, *Pres., NYCTA*	Daniel T. Scannell, *1st Vice Chair*
Montreal Urban Community Transit Corporation	Louise Roy, *Pres., GM*	Robert Perreault, *Chair*
New Jersey Transit Corporation	Shirley A. DeLibero, *Exec. Dir.*	Thomas M. Downs, *Chair*
Port Authority of Allegheny County	William W. Millar, *Exec. Dir.*	John P. Robin, *Chair*
Port Authority Trans-Hudson Corporation	Richard R. Kelly, *VP, GM*	
Sacramento Regional Transit District	Thomas G. Matoff, *GM*	Lynn Robie, *Chair*
San Diego Metropolitan Transit Development Board	Thomas F. Larwin, *GM*	James R. Mills, *Chair*
San Francisco Bay Area Rapid Transit District	Frank J. Wilson, *GM*	Nello Bianco, *Dir.*
Santa Clara County Transportation Agency	Lawrence G. Reuter, *Dir.*	Rod Diridon, *Chair*
Southeastern Pennsylvania Transportation Authority	Louis J. Gambaccini, *GM, Chief Opr. Ofc.*	J. Clayton Undercofler, *Chair*
Southern California Rapid Transit District	Alan F. Pegg, *GM*	Nikolas Patsaouras, *Pres.*
Toronto Transit Commission	Allan F. Leach, *Chief GM*	
Tri-County Metropolitan Transportation District of Oregon	Thomas J. Walsh, *GM*	Loren L. Wyss, *Pres.*
Washington Metropolitan Area Transit Authority	David L. Gunn, *GM*	Joseph Alexander, *Bd. Member*

APTA Regional Directors

Region I --- Maine, Vermont, New Hampshire, Massachusetts, Connecticut, New York and Rhode Island

Capital District Transportation Authority	Dennis J. Fitzgerald, *Exec. Dir.*	Robert G. Lyman, *Chair*
Connecticut Transit	Robert D. Lorah, *GM*	James F. Byrnes, Jr., *Dpty. Comm.*
Metropolitan Suburban Bus Authority	L. A. Kimball, *GM*	
Rochester-Genesee Regional Transportation Authority	John A. Garrity, *Exec. Dir., GM*	Andrew F. Caverly, *Chair*

Region II --- New Jersey, Pennsylvania, Delaware, Maryland, Virginia, West Virginia, Washington, DC, North Carolina and South Carolina

Berks Area Reading Transportation Authority	Dennis D. Louwerse, *Exec. Dir.*	Michael Roeberg, *Chair*
Charlotte Transit System	David A. Hines, *GM*	Sue Myrick, *Mayor*
Lehigh and Northampton Transportation Authority	Armando V. Greco, *Exec. Dir.*	Denise M. von Funk, *Chair*
Montgomery County Ride-On	Gordon A. Aoyagi, *Chief*	Robert S. McGarry, *Dir.*

Region III --- Kentucky, Tennessee, Georgia, Florida, Alabama, Mississippi, Arkansas, Louisiana, Puerto Rico and U.S. Virgin Islands

Hillsborough Area Regional Transit Authority	Sharon Dent, *Exec. Dir.*	Robert A. Darr, *Chair*
Regional Transit Authority	Wayne A. Dupre, *Exec. Dir.*	Kern A. Reese, Esq., *Chair*
Memphis Area Transit Authority	Fred M. Gilliam, *GM*	Samuel P. Rabb, *Vice Chair*
Metropolitan Transit Authority	Robert T. Babbitt, *GM*	R.C.H. Mathews, III, *Chair*

Region IV --- Minnesota, Wisconsin, Illinois, Indiana, Ohio, Michigan, North Dakota and South Dakota

Champaign-Urbana Mass Transit District	William L. Volk, *Mng. Dir.*	
Duluth Transit Authority	Dennis Jensen, *GM*	Alan Mettner, *Pres.*
Miami Valley Regional Transit Authority	Forest D. Swift, *Exec. Dir.*	George W. Chamberlain, *Pres.*
Milwaukee County Transit System	Thomas P. Kujawa, *Mng. Dir.*	Lawrence J. Kenny, *Chair*

APTA Regional Directors

Region V --- Nebraska, Kansas, Oklahoma, Texas, Montana, Wyoming, Colorado, Utah, New Mexico, Iowa and Missouri

Fort Worth Transportation Authority	John P. Bartosiewicz, *GM*	Hershel R. Payne, *Chair*
Kansas City Area Transportation Authority	Richard F. Davis, *GM*	Howard C. Breen, *Chair*
Metropolitan Tulsa Transit Authority	Mark I. Pritchard, *GM*	Robert O. Laird, *Trustee*
Topeka Metropolitan Transit Authority	Craig O. Cole, *GM*	Edward M. Fallon, *Chair*

Region VI --- Idaho, Nevada, Arizona, Washington, Oregon, California, Alaska and Hawaii

Fresno Transit	Terry O. Cooper, *Dir.*	
San Mateo County Transit District	Gerald T. Haugh, *GM*	
Riverside Transit Agency	Susan J. Hafner, *GM*	Dick Deininger, *Chair*
Sun Tran	Bruce Behncke, *GM*	Thomas J. Volgy, *Mayor*

Region VII --- Canada

BC Transit	M. J. O'Connor, *Pres., CEO*	
Edmonton Transit	Gregory R. Latham, *Mgr.*	John Schnablegger, *GM*
The Hamilton Street Railway Company	Dale Turvey, *GM*	
Calgary Transit	Robert Irwin, *GM*	R. Magnus, *Alderman*

APTA Associate Member Directors

ABB Traction Inc.	Ake Wennberg, *Sr. VP*
The Flxible Corporation	Mark J. Obert, *Vice Chair*
Hausman Bus Sales	Bill J. Chaddock, *Exec. VP*
LUMINATOR	David L. Turney, *CEO*
Robinson and Associates	Claude G. Robinson, *Pres.*
Smith & Howard Associates, Inc.	Irving P. Smith, *Pres.*
Transportation Manufacturing Corporation	John R. Nasi, *Pres. & CEO*
VAPOR	James A. Machesney, *VP*
WABCO	John M. Meister, *VP & GM*
Frank Zarider	Frank Zarider, *Principal*

APTA Honorary Members

John C. Baine	John L. McDonnell
Edgar F. Claffey	Eugene M. Barnes
F. Norman Hill	David F. Girard-diCarlo
S. A. Caria	Leonard Ronis
Robert T. Pollock	James H. Graebner
Stanley H. Gates, Jr.	Joseph Alexander
Dr. William J. Ronan	Bernard J. Ford, Sr.
James J. McDonough	Warren H. Frank
Thomas O. Prior	Laurence W. Jackson
Harold L. Fisher	Reba Malone
Houston P. Ishmael	James E. Cowen

San Francisco Bay Area
Metropolitan Transportation Commission

Santa Clara County Transit District
Board of Supervisors

Most sincere appreciation is conveyed to the following donors whose generous support for rail transit has made this publication possible.

ENGINEERS

Bechtel
Mel Mirsky, Vice President and Manager,
Surface Transportation
(415) 768-3660

Parsons Brinckerhoff Quade & Douglas, Inc.
Michael I. Schneider, West Group Manager
(714) 973-4880

Mark IV Transportation Products Group
David L. Turney, Group Executive
(214) 516-3129

UTDC Corporation
Bob Furniss, President
(313) 642-6600

CONDUCTORS

Institutue for National Surface
Transportation Policy Studies (INSTPS)
Marshall Burak, Dean, San Jose State
University School of Business
(408) 924-3400

Los Angeles County
Transportation Commission
Neil Peterson, Executive Director
(213) 623-1194

Smith Barney, Harris Upham & Co. Inc.
Frank Chin, Executive Vice President and
Transportation Group Manager
(212) 698-6101

FIREMEN

ABB Traction, Inc.
Lutz W. Elsner,
President
(607) 732-5251

General Motors Locomotive Group, General
Motors Corporation
Bruce B. Johnson, Sales Manager,
Passenger Locomotives
(519) 452-5117

ICF Kaiser Engineers, Inc.
Gerald V. Gibney, Vice President
(415) 268-6000

Bank of America NT&SA,
Public Finance Department
Thomas F. Opdycke, Vice President and
Managing Director
(415) 953-5439

Gibbs & Hill
Peter Mazza,
President
(212) 216-6000

LTK Engineering Services
J. Richard Tomlinson,
President
(215) 542-0700

Bombardier Corporation
William D. Lochte, General Manager,
Marketing & Sales (U.S.)
(215) 639-1444

Grigsby Brandford Powell Inc.
Napoleon Brandford, Executive Vice President
(415) 392-4800

Morrison Knudsen Corporation
Anthony Daniels,
Vice President, Transportation
(415) 442-7474

Daniel, Mann, Johnson, & Mendenhall (DMJM)
Gerald W. Seelman,
Corporate Vice President
(213) 381-3663

Harmon Industries Inc.
Robert G. Clawson, Vice President,
Sales and Marketing
(816) 229-3345

O'Brien-Kreitzberg & Associates
Larry Hazzard, Senior Vice President
(818) 907-6666

De Leuw, Cather & Company
Gary E. Griggs, Senior Vice President
(202) 775-3331

Hatch Associates
Gordon A. Smith, Senior Vice President,
Transportation
(416) 855-7600

Orrick, Herrington & Sutcliffe
Mary A. Collins, Partner
(415) 773-5998

High-Point Schaer
Joel Callahan, General Manager,
Los Angeles
(213) 486-9884

BRAKEMEN

A&K Railroad Materials
Morris Kulmer, President (801) 974-5484

LS Transit Systems, Inc.
A. P. Engel, President
(201) 893-6000

Introduction

by Alan F. Kiepper, Chair, APTA Board of Directors
President, New York City Transit Authority

This book was prepared to establish a vantage point from which to view the development of rail transit in the coming decade. As Chairman of the American Public Transit Association, the successor to the first street railway association founded 109 years ago in Boston, I commend the San Francisco Bay Area Metropolitan Transportation Commission, the Santa Clara County Transportation Agency, and Rod Diridon, APTA Vice President - Rail Transit, for bringing this book to fruition.

New York City Transit Authority

Rail transit in North America is a story of cities and the need for mobility of a large labor force and the growth of a dynamic economy and population. From the first recorded operation of horse-drawn coaches in the early nineteenth century to the inauguration of fully automated transit systems, rail transit connects the central cities internally to the suburbs and to points for extended trips.

The story of rail transit begins with laying of track and the use of horse propulsion in the era from the 1830s to the 1880s. Toward the end of that period several changes in

Government of Ontario Transit

took place. First was the use of rails and flanged wheels. The second change provided an external power source to replace the familiar one or two horse teams that pulled the cars.

Cable traction introduced the first form of external power. This technology is forever associated with inventor Andrew Hallidie and the City of San Francisco which began its first cable railway service in 1873. Many other cities quickly followed by installing this unique form of propulsion.

Whereas cable traction had obvious advantages in the famous hills of San Francisco, it's interesting to note that the largest cable traction system was installed in Chicago, a city noted more for its wind than for its hills. A cable railway even ran across the fabled Brooklyn Bridge. A footnote on the passing of cable traction is that even though Chicago had the world's largest cable system, horse car routes were still in service after the cable system was abandoned.

With public transit firmly on rails, the long sought after goal of self-propelled rail cars became possible due in large part to the genius and efforts of Frank Sprague. Sprague is credited with creating and producing the first practical and successful electrically propelled rail system in Richmond, Virginia in 1888. His contract required that he provide the entire railway including trackage, traction power and streetcars.

Richmond became a technology model for the huge street railway and electric interurbans that provided the great bulk of public transportation into the 1920s. Within a few years of the Richmond System installation, electric traction eclipsed cable traction as new electric systems were installed and cable and horse car routes were converted to electric traction. In the mid-1930s the classic streetcar appeared, the "PCC", named after the transit industry committee (President's Conference Committee) that guided its design. Streetcar operations today are known as "light rail" systems.

As street railways grew, the problem of limited street space restricted the speed of streetcars. Several cities looked skyward. First in New York and later in Chicago the construction of elevated railways progressed. At first, the propulsion systems followed that of the streetcar with use of cable traction and a major intervening step of using steam power. The major New York and Chicago elevated railroads employed small steam locomotives and coaches to provide passenger service. Steam was used for only a short time — electric propulsion soon became the norm with powered cars and trailers.

10

Metro North Commuter Railroad

The major defect of this powercar-trailer method was decreased performance as more trailers were added. The solution was the introduction of multiple unit control systems. This allowed one motorman to control identical powered cars in trains of one to ten cars. This great invention, demonstrated in Chicago in 1898, was due to the same man who introduced electric traction to streetcars — the ubiquitous Frank Sprague.

Elevated railroads came only to the more densely populated major U.S. cities. Since they were a far better form of transit than street operations, due to much higher average speeds, they became a major mover of people in central cities.

Near the start of the twentieth century, as New York and Chicago looked up to find a way to speed passengers over city streets, Boston became the first city to look down. The first transit subway was designed for streetcars and opened in Boston in 1897. New York began subway construction in 1900 and opened its first line in 1904. In the first half of the twentieth century, Chicago and Philadelphia followed suit.

These subways usually connected with elevated routes that fit the needs of geography and cities. The combination of elevated and subway operations, now called heavy rail, forever freed the electric railway from the restraints of street operation. Average speeds of elevated/subway lines are two to three times faster than streetcars. The magic of a fast, smooth ride via rail transit became a major marketing factor.

Streetcars, elevateds and subways became tools of the central city. Steam railroads connecting outer areas to inner cities is now termed commuter service, and is both the oldest and newest rail transit service. Commuter rail transit is alive and well as we head into the 21st century with twelve cities having this mode of rail transit.

The blending of rail guideway technology and electric propulsion has produced the reality of a transit system offering safe, fast, clean service with minimum human intervention. Automated guideway transit (AGT) has proven to be effective in large scale use in Vancouver and Miami. Many different technologies are available for the future. The control systems used on these systems are similar to those employed in San Francisco and Washington, D.C. and represent a full system concept, that of station access, fare collection and train operations with these functions controlled by computer technology. A careful blending of control and backup systems insures safety and security.

The Texas Triangle's proposed TGV Atlantique

In Canada, technical developments followed similar patterns; street railways using horse cars, conversion to electric operations, adoption of commuter, heavy rail and automated systems. Only Toronto has retained streetcars while building a heavy rail system and reestablishing a regional commuter rail system. In Montreal the heavy rail system uses electricity for propulsion and rubber tires for support, and a large regional commuter rail system is operated as well. Canada has also established two new light rail systems and an elevated/subway automated guideway system using a unique linear induction motor drive.

Rail is definitely a preferred mode. In 1960 there were ten North American cities with commuter, heavy rail or light rail (streetcar) operations. In 1991 there are 29 cities, a 190% increase. In addition there are more than 40 cities actively planning or studying the construction of rail transit. It is conceivable, even likely, that over 40 cities could be operating rail transit by the beginning of the 21st century.

With the U.S. and Canada facing problems of gridlock and air pollution, the twin technologies of rail guidance and electric propulsion are obvious answers to myriad national problems in urban areas. At present, over 30% of all public transit passengers are carried by vehicles propelled by electricity. Transit is far ahead of other passenger modes in the use of non-petroleum fuels.

The following pages illustrate the need to provide greater financial support to a rapidly growing demand for rail transit in North America.

Foreword

by Rod Diridon, Vice President, APTA Rail Transit
Chair, Santa Clara County Transit District Board of Supervisors

Santa Clara County Transportation Agency's Guadalupe Corridor Light Rail Line

The world is changing more rapidly than ever before. The 21st century will be far more different from the 20th than that century was from its predecessor. We will simultaneously be using the bounty of our vast technological innovations while fighting for the environmental life of our planet.

A key element in that technological solution will be the evolution of North American mass transportation. It is appropriate that the transition decade during which these phenomenal changes will begin is the 1990s; the last decade of the old millennium. Some in our society will resist these changes, attempting to protect the status quo for the same regressive social and economic reasons that have prompted stagnation in the past. The American transit industry, as represented by the American Public Transit Association, is in the forefront of those embracing change for the sake of a better future. Transit leaders throughout North America recognize that continued overuse of the single-passenger automobile is causing the destruction of our environmental and economic systems. According to research done by General Manager Lou Gambaccini at the Southeastern Pennsylvania Transportation Authority, the vehicle miles traveled in the U.S. during the 1980s outpaced population growth by a rate of four to one. A continuation of this trend over the next century spells disaster.

The result has been highway congestion to the point of impassibility during commute hours, stifling economic prosperity in virtually all of our most dynamic metropolitan areas. Air pollution in every major metropolitan area in the United States is at levels significantly exceeding those identified as healthy for our children and theirs. To fuel this degradation of our lifestyle, we're importing more than 50% of our oil — by far the largest contributor to the U.S. deficit balance of trade. In only a few decades, the United States has been transformed from the largest creditor to the largest debtor nation in the world.

The solution that, over time, will reduce vehicle miles traveled, traffic congestion, air pollution and our demand for foreign oil is a comprehensive, integrated and safe national mass transportation system. And in our major metropolitan areas, where the vast majority of the population lives and works, the most efficient mode of mass transportation is rail transit.

United States rail transportation systems now in operation were generally built in the early to mid part of this century. With few exceptions, the systems have not been maintained, updated or expanded to meet growing demands. The Federal Reserve Bank of Chicago recently found a direct correlation between national investments in infrastructure and increase in gross national product. The study indicates that during the 1970s and 1980s the United States averaged less than one half of one percent of our gross domestic product per annum invested in infrastructure. Consequently we averaged less than a one percent GNP increase during the same time. All other industrialized countries of the world far exceed the United States in each category, with Japan investing over five percent per annum and increasing productivity well over three percent. West Germany, Italy, France, the United Kingdom and Canada follow closely behind. Not coincidentally, the tax on motor vehicle fuel in every other industrialized country is three to seven times higher than the U.S. motor vehicle fuel tax. That higher taxing strategy not only creates the revenue to invest in fine mass transportation systems, but it also discourages overuse of the single-passenger vehicle and excessive importation of foreign oil.

Congress' passage of the 1990 Clean Air Act and the 1991 federal five-cent increase in motor vehicle fuel tax signal the beginning of a transition to transportation systems designed, constructed and funded in a manner more consistent with the other industrialized countries of the world. And it is fortuitous that, as we transition into a new era of rail and guideway transit, the technology of those modes is evolving dramatically.

So as we begin to concentrate on reconstructing and expanding our rail transit systems, we will have a menu of modes available that were not dreamed of only a few years ago. Ultra high-speed bullet trains like the French TGV, the German ICE, the Swedish T-200 and others available now may evolve within ten to twenty years into an even faster and more economical magnetically levitated, linearly accelerated (maglev) system being tested by Germany and Japan. Even though high-speed rail and maglev were originally invented in the United States, we will have to purchase that technology from abroad because the U.S. government neglected to financially support the transit research and development programs so aggressively pursued by German and Japanese public and private investors.

There are, of course, many fringe benefits — beyond congestion, air pollution and trade deficit reduction — to a rail-based transportation system. Rail systems encourage compact growth around rail stations, thereby discouraging urban sprawl which threatens to devour our farm land and open space and exacerbates excessive fuel use. Further, rail transportation creates employment, not only during the construction period, but also for the many transit professionals who operate newly built systems.

So it is time, during this transition decade, to aggressively pursue the transit systems that will allow us to survive and prosper in the 21st century. Any further delay could, at worst, prove terminal to life on earth and, at best, leave us at a disadvantage as we attempt to move employees, goods and services in an increasingly competitive world economy.

This book describes our rail transportation system embryo with its current capacities, phenomenal potential and crying financial need. Our fervent hope is that the reader will realize the potential, respond to the need and find the resources to spark the transition.

Transrapid's German maglev prototype

Great appreciation must be offered to the project team that worked so hard, in such a short period of time, to publish the book. Chairman Alan Kiepper, Executive Vice President Jack Gilstrap, Deputy Executive Vice President Frank Cihak and all of the officers, staff and members of the American Public Transit Association must be complimented for their leadership into this new transit era. Special thanks to APTA Affiliate Vice President David Turney and the affiliate members for their funding support which has been recognized on a special page in the book. Also special appreciation to Larry Dahms, Executive Director and staff of the San Francisco Bay Area Metropolitan Transportation Commission; and to General Manager Larry Reuter and staff of the Santa Clara County Transportation Agency for their technical advice and encouragement. But the heart of this book has been Project Director Colleen Crowley, Graphics Manager Rick Kitson, Project Assistant Jan Perez, Susan Fitts, my Executive Assistant who insured quality control, and Technical Information Directors Brent Cardwell, Nancy Toledo and Paul Ogren. Great appreciation also goes to San Jose State University President Gail Fullerton and Business School Dean Marshall Burak for providing support to this project through the Institute for National Surface Transportation Policy Studies (INSTPS) at San Jose State University. These and other team members from my staff and the staff of the Santa Clara County Transportation Agency gave the thousands of extra hours that have allowed this project to evolve from concept to published page in less than six months.

The national need for a transition to transit is clear. Leaders at the national, state, regional and local levels have the means to meet the need. The public is ready for and demanding an emphasis on transit. The remaining question? Have we the courage to break out of our highway-bound status quo, embrace change, and create the funds to buy the rails that will guarantee mobility, clean air and energy independence for the 21st century?

Chicago Transit Authority

NORTH AMERICAN RAIL TRANSIT

SUMMARY OF RAIL SYSTEMS

Survey Explanation

Information in this publication is based on responses by 50 U.S. and Canadian rail operators surveyed by APTA. The surveys are printed in full beginning on page 33. Preceding the survey data is summary information which begins on the following page.

In order to determine funding needs for current and planned rail projects, rail transit systems were asked to project all major planned capital projects, whether or not federal, state or local funding was expected to be available. The intent was to show a comprehensive need picture not artificially restricted by current funding levels. Systems were asked to include any projects which could require funding before the year 2000. Following are notes on the data surveys which appear later in the book.

GENERAL SURVEY NOTES

Annual figures are shown by fiscal year (FY).

All ridership and financial figures are given in thousands, i.e., if the FY 1990 figure is 1,000,000, "1,000" is entered in the appropriate survey box.

Unless otherwise noted, financial projections are based on a 5% per year inflation rate.

When "N/A" (not available) or blank survey boxes appear, the data was not provided to APTA by the surveyed rail system.

SURVEY ELEMENTS

1. **Rail Ridership**: Annual total boardings (rail only).

2. **Rail System Employees**: Total number of full-time equivalent employees (FTE's) assigned to the rail operation. Both direct and overhead labor are included.

3. **Track Miles**: Total miles of revenue and service track. Double and single track are noted in the "Comments" section. Yard track is excluded.

4. **Number of Rail Vehicles**: Total number of rail vehicles, including spares.

5. **Annual Capital Budget**: Capital projections for existing and planned rail including the cost of major vehicle overhauls and support facilities (i.e. maintenance).

6. **Annual Operating Budget**: Total direct and overhead operating costs for rail.

7. **Total Rail Budget**: Sum of Annual Capital Budget and Annual Operating Budget.

8. **Portion of Rail Budget Paid with Federal Funds (based on current law)**:
   Operating: Maximum portion of rail operating budget which could be paid with federal funds, such as UMTA Section 9 funds.
   Capital: Maximum portion of capital budget which could be paid with federal funds, whether or not funds are expected to be received. Capital funding figures for 2000 and Projected 10-year total should be 75% of the capital budget, reflecting the maximum allowable under the current law.
   Total: Sum of maximum allowable capital subsidy and maximum allowable operating subsidy.
   Note: In Canadian properties, figures reflect provincial rather than federal subsibies.

1985 and 1990 Columns: Entries represent actual money spent or received rather than budgeted or expected.

2000 Column: Entries represent estimated annual totals for the year 2000 only.

Projected 10-Year Total Column: Entries represent cumulative totals (i.e. FY 1991 figure + FY 1992 figure, adding each year's figure through FY 2000).

Rail Funding: A Statement of Need

The following pages contain data for 44 U.S. and six Canadian rail systems. There is also summary data for both countries. Amtrak is a separately funded national system and is, therefore, not included in U.S. national summary data. In the case of joint operations, data have been tallied only once to avoid double counting for the same system. In addition to the 50 systems surveyed in the United States and Canada, over 40 cities listed below are considering rail transit and many could begin construction in the next decade. They range from having plans to place measures to fund transit studies and projects on the ballot to being ready to begin construction. Their early stage plans preclude providing reliable data at this point. The rail needs projected here are, therefore, very conservative estimates, since they do not include potential new systems, especially the intercity rail lines, that could double the projected capital and operating need.

With the noted exceptions for which projections were not available, this APTA survey yields a total U.S. rail transit capital cost between 1991 and 2000 of over $81 billion. If the federal government were to fund 75%, as required by the 1987 Surface Transportation Act, the federal subsidy for rail transit required from 1991-2000 would be almost $61 billion. But in practice, the Urban Mass Transit Administration requires, in most cases, more than a 25% local match before a grant will be considered. Many local agencies, therefore, are providing much more than the 25% in local matching funds. When this "overmatch" occurs, other local transit capital requirements are then not covered.   When asked for the maximum federal capital subsidy available according to the current law, the response of those surveyed totals over $53 billion. Because overmatching has become a routine practice so strongly encouraged by UMTA, the federal funding actually received by the properties is much less than this.

The APTA survey reveals operating costs of U.S. rail transit systems in the next ten years to be almost $73 billion. The systems indicated the maximum federal operating subsidy they expected to receive is about $2 billion. Many transit agencies with both rail and bus operations do not separately calculate rail farebox recovery percentages. Therefore, a reliable calculation of user fee cost recovery is not available. General estimates indicate that over 30% of operating costs will not be covered by fares. If the federal government provided 50% of this operating deficit, per the 1987 Surface Transportation Reauthorization Act, the amount would be far greater than the $2 billion indicated by the agencies. This suggests that national transportation planning is being artificially constrained by the lack of operating subsidy that would be available if operating assistance were provided at a level envisioned during the 1987 Surface Transportation Act Reauthorization.

As mentioned above, many cities with planned and existing rail have not been included because they were not yet able to project reliable data. Cities not included in this publication with existing or planned small operations, mostly historic trolleys, include Aspen, Detroit, Dubuque, Fort Collins, Fort Smith, Frederick, Galveston, Irving, Lowell, Minneapolis, Nelson, Niagara Falls, Quebec City, Rockford and Yakima.

The following cities have planned rail operations — mostly light rail, but some commuter rail and people movers — and have not provided data for the publication: Austin, Brunswick, Burlington, Charleston, Charlotte, Cincinnati, Columbus, Hamilton, Harrisburg, Hartford, Indianapolis, Kansas City, Memphis, Milwaukee, Nashville, Norfolk, Oklahoma City, Orlando, Phoenix, Raleigh, Richmond, Rochester, St. Paul, Salt Lake City, Seattle, Tampa Bay and Tucson.

Potential intercity corridors for which data was not yet available for this publication are Atlanta-Macon-Savannah, Brunswick-Bath, Cleveland-Columbus-Cincinnati, Dallas-San Antonio-Austin-Houston, Detroit-Chicago-St. Louis-Kansas City-Indianapolis-Cincinnati, Los Angeles-Phoenix, New York-Albany-Buffalo-Montreal, Minneapolis-Chicago-Detroit, Orlando-Tampa, Philadelphia-Harrisburg-Pittsburgh, Portland-Seattle-Vancouver, Pueblo-Colorado Springs-Denver-Fort Collins, Quebec City-Windsor, Reno-Las Vegas-Phoenix, Sacramento-San Francisco Bay Area- Los Angeles-San Diego, and Santa Fe-Albuquerque.

In the following pages are an explanation of the survey data, locations of the surveyed rail operations, national summaries, property by property summaries and individual property synopses listed alphabetically by state or province.

North American

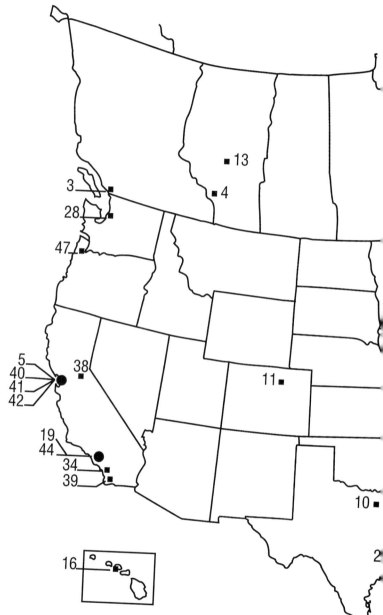

■ Represents single property

● Represents multiple properties

Rail Systems

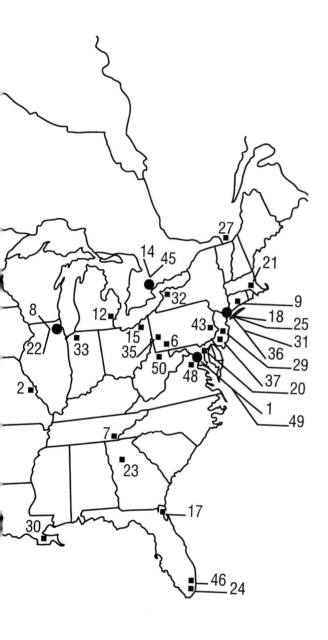

UNITED STATES MASS TRANSIT NEEDS: 1990-2000

Data For Rail Operations	1990	2000	10-Year Projected Total
Rail Ridership	2,277,908	2,958,265	25,396,204
Track Miles	8,208	9,795	
Number of Vehicles *(All Types)*:			
In Operation	16,345	19,682	
Refurbished	1,005	1,797	5,158
Replaced	0	685	2,746
Total Rail Capital Cost	$4,493,841	$8,102,940	$81,233,885
Total Rail Operating Cost	$5,383,053	$9,278,244	$72,901,499
Total Rail Cost	$9,876,894	$17,381,184	$154,135,384
Data for Bus Operations			
Bus Ridership	6,000,000	8,300,000	71,500,000
Number of Buses:			
In Operation	81,000	111,500	
Refurbished	2,025	3,100	31,000
Replaced	6,075	9,800	98,000
Total Bus Capital Cost	$1,400,000	$8,600,000	$43,600,000
Total Bus Operating Cost	$9,700,000	$15,800,000	$128,100,000
Total Bus Cost	$11,100,000	$24,400,000	$171,700,000
Total Transit Cost	$20,976,894	$41,781,184	$325,835,384
Federal Contribution (Deficit)			
Portion of Rail Cost That Would Be Paid With Federal Funds if Available (Based on Current Law):			
Capital	$1,552,572	$5,043,640	$53,426,004
Operating	$180,892	$250,806	$2,021,538
Total	$1,733,464	$5,294,446	$55,447,542
Portion of Bus Cost That Would Be Paid With Federal Funds if Available (Based on Current Law):			
Capital	$1,050,000	$6,450,000	$32,700,000
Operating	$3,307,700	$5,387,800	$43,682,100
Total	$4,357,700	$11,837,800	$76,382,100
Portion of Total Transit Cost That Would Be Paid With Federal Funds if Available (Based on Current Law)	$6,091,164	$17,132,246	$131,829,642
Total Federal Contribution Based on Current Funding Levels	$3,200,000	$5,200,000	$42,300,000
Total Federal Funding Shortfall	$2,891,164	$11,932,246	$89,529,642

NOTE: Ridership and financial data in thousands, add (000). Track miles in this table are single track. Rail data based on sum totals of projections by 43 U.S. rail systmes surveyed by APTA. Amtrak has not been included in this data summary because it

U.S. MASS TRANSIT FEDERAL FUNDING DEFICIT ($000's)

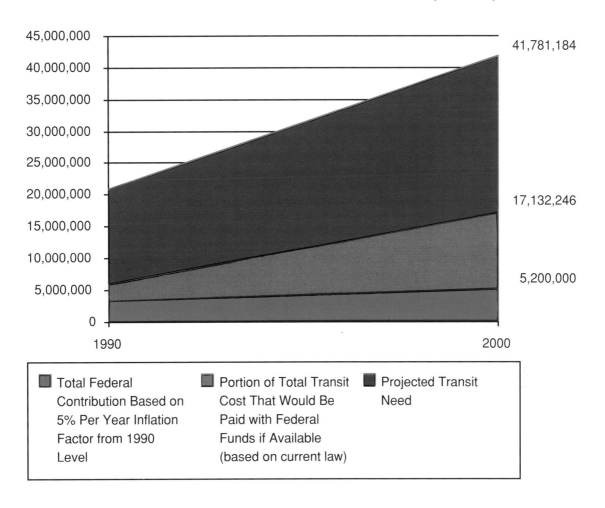

Legend:
- Total Federal Contribution Based on 5% Per Year Inflation Factor from 1990 Level
- Portion of Total Transit Cost That Would Be Paid with Federal Funds if Available (based on current law)
- Projected Transit Need

NOTE (cont.)

s a national system and funded separately from local transit programs. For information about Amtrak, see page 32. Over 40 dditional cities are considering rail transit systems (for a listing, see page 19), but do not yet have data reliable enough for this ublication. Many of those are likely to begin construction before 2000 and will significantly add to the needs projected in this able. For a full explanation of the federal funding deficit, see page 19.

Canadian Mass Transit Summary

Canadian mass transportation operators do not project ridership and financial needs in the same manner required of United States operators. Therefore, instead of a table illustrating ten-year trends as was prepared for the United States mass transit industry, a narrative describing the Canadian transportation programs is being provided.

The data presented have been provided by the Canadian Urban Transit Association of Toronto. GO Transit's Chairman Lou Parsons, who is currently Vice Chairman of the Board of the American Public Transit Association and just nominated to be Chairman, also advised in the preparation of this section. The information is based primarily on 1988-89 actual trends which are somewhat sparse for reliable extrapolation. Summary data for the six Canadian transit systems responding to the survey are presented on page 26 in the property-by-property summary.

In the late 1980s the Canadian mass transportation industry was shrinking slightly. The number of light and heavy rail vehicles in operation increased during this period but total vehicle kilometers traveled declined. Heavy rail vehicle kilometers dropped from 138.2 million to 136.5 million, while that of light rail dropped from 35.9 million to 34.0 million. The total vehicle kilometers traveled, including buses and other conveyances, dropped from 771.8 million to 752.6 million.

During the same period of 1988-1989, revenue passengers declined from 1.54 billion to 1.52 billion. Because of fare increases, which may have contributed to the ridership drop, the total operating revenue increased from $1.16 to $1.25 billion Canadian dollars. This increased revenue was more than offset by an increase in total operating costs of $2.43 billion to $2.62 billion Canadian dollars. As a result of the higher operating deficit, subsidy from municipalities and provincial sources each increased with the latter contributing the lion's share of the additional required revenue.

Contrasting with this trend and offering great hope for the long-term future of Canadian transit is an upward movement in capital expenditures from $447.8 million in 1988 to $599.5 million in 1989. The majority of that increase was invested in new rolling stock which will undoubtedly result in higher ridership figures and increased operating efficiency in the future. To cover these additional capital expenditures, contributions from municipalities rose dramatically along with the provincial contribution.

An examination of the rail transit experience of major Canadian transit operators indicates a recent upturn in ridership and a longer-term intent to dramatically expand urban mass transit facilities, especially in communities like Toronto. The reader is encouraged to examine the Canadian portion of this book beginning on page 121 to gain greater insight into these operations.

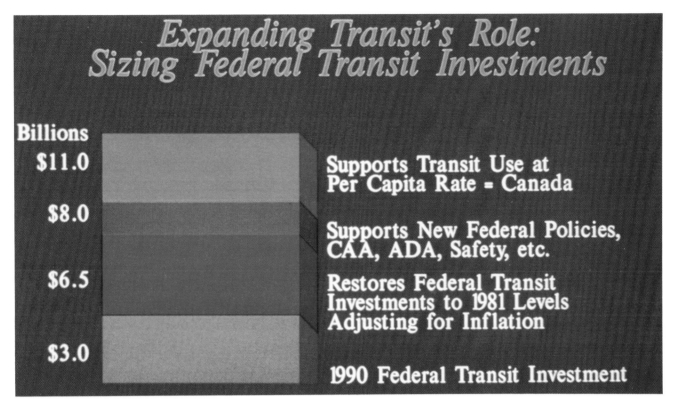

If transit funding had merely kept pace with the inflation of the 1980s, APTA's U.S. core transit program of $6.5 billion would be funded. To accommodate mandated programs and increase transit use, annual federal funding needs to increase to $11 billion which equals the per capita transit investment by Canada.

AVERAGE PRODUCTIVITY GROWTH PER ANNUM
PUBLIC INVESTMENT AND PRODUCTIVITY, 1973-1985

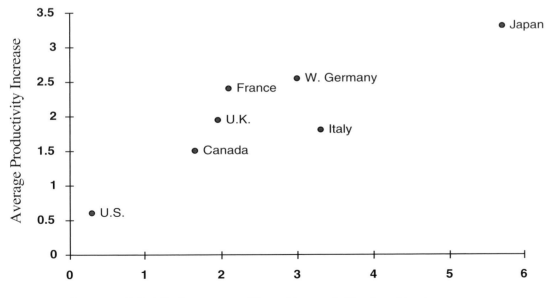

Average % Public Investment/Gross Domestic Product Per Annum

Compared to the other G-7 (major) industrialized nations, U.S. and Canadian low levels of investment in public infrastructure correlate to very low productivity growth rates. Competitors, realizing the benefits of public capital investment, enjoyed strong productivity gains. Between 1973 and 1985, the average U.S. investment in public infrastructure was 0.3% of gross domestic product, while American productivity growth was only 0.6%. The Japanese invested over 5% of their gross domestic product in public capital, and Japanese productivity grew at a 3.3% clip.

Source: David Ashauer, Federal Reserve Bank of Chicago

Financial Needs Summary

USA

	Annual Ridership 1990	Total Capital Budget 1990
Amtrak	22,187	$202,700
Bi-State Development Agency (Missouri)	0	$121,333
California Department of Transportation	6,400	$32,131
Cambria County Transit Authority	205	$2,213
Chattanooga Area Regional Transportation Authority	358	$84
Chicago Transit Authority	166,757	$390,734
Connecticut Department of Transportation	16,309	$58,217
Dallas Area Rapid Transit	—	—
Denver Regional Transportation District	—	—
Detroit Department of Transportation	24.4	$0
Greater Cleveland Regional Transit Authority	8,891	$38,704
Honolulu Department of Transportation	—	—
Jacksonville Transportation Authority	399	$8,432
Long Island Rail Road	72,359	$208,700
Los Angeles County Transportation Commission	—	—
Mass Transit Administration of Maryland	17,068	$155,943
Massachusetts Bay Transportation Authority	192,300	$383,710
Metra (Chicago)	72,000	$111,731
Metro Atlanta Rapid Transit Authority	68,947	$94,818
Metro-Dade Transit Agency (Miami)	13,622	$2,651
Metro-North Commuter Railroad (New York)	57,641	$171,000
Metropolitan Transit Authority (Houston)	—	—
Municipality of Metropolitan Seattle	149	$6,544
New Jersey Transit Corporation	41,833	$183,558
New Orleans Regional Transit Authority	8,346	$47,000
New York City Transit Authority	1,027,936	$1,184,000
Niagara Frontier Transportation Authority	8,480	$2,686
No. Indiana Commuter Transportation District	3,475	$21,000

* All figures in thousands (add 000)

Total Operating Budget 1990	Total Capital Requirements Next 10yrs	Total Operating Requirements Next 10yrs	Federal Subsidy Requirements Next 10yrs
$2,011,800	$5,400,000	$11,769,030	$3,631,129
$0	$1,134,434	$109,300	$953,876
$28,561	$1,377,270	$300,000	$443,190
$216	$1,200	$2,500	$1,500
$676	$1,875	$8,681	$3,236
$278,905	$5,134,470	$3,694,000	$4,047,000
$111,914	$1,856,600	$1,558,783	$1,447,000
—	$1,759,600	$1,500,000	$330,000
—	$67,300	$17,048	$0
$350	$500	$3,500	$0
$23,210	$557,161	$369,623	$468,276
—	$1,241,000	$105,600	$945,150
$617	$135,000	$14,000	$101,250
$611,500	$1,769,700	$4,947,500	$522,709
—	$12,053,000	$1,395,000	$8,600,000
$40,491	$762,322	$578,370	$434,476
$353,246	$8,461,470	$4,665,240	$6,466,502
$315,126	$1,802,000	$4,103,763	$552,580
$60,708	$867,909	$952,121	$679,939
$43,632	$1,377,881	$608,644	$436,676
$481,068	$2,476,000	$6,812,800	$1,937,000
—	$1,089,793	$38,854	$544,897
$762	$156,544	$13,347	$25,000
$283,600	$3,866,670	$3,965,100	$3,078,702
$3,990	$299,000	$14,000	$226,990
$1,743,400	$15,008,000	$20,500,000	$11,871,000
$11,806	$400,000	$160,000	$315,250
$23,500	$85,000	$295,000	$92,250

USA (continued)

	Annual Ridership 1990	Total Capital Budget 1990
No. San Diego County Transit Development Board	—	—
Port Authority of Allegheny County	9,840	$2,859
Port Authority Trans-Hudson Corporation (New York)	56,000	$168,000
Port Authority Transit Corporation (Penn. & N.J.)	11,405	$10,725
Sacramento Regional Transit District	5,700	$5,200
San Diego Metro Transit Development Board	15,500	$50,000
San Francisco Bay Area Rapid Transit District	74,761	$129,278
San Francisco Municipal Railway	49,403	$36,000
Santa Clara County Transportation Agency	3,600	$2,000
SE Pennsylvania Transportation Authority	110,411	$294,000
Southern California Rapid Transit District	6,500	$350,000
Tri-County Commuter Rail Authority (Florida)	1,419	$283,500
Tri-County Metro Transportation District of Oregon	6,720	$79,068
Virginia Railway Express	2,250	$6,700
Washington Metro Area Transit Authority	145,000	$201,192
West Virginia University, Morgantown PRT	2,400	$130

Canada

	Annual Ridership 1990	Total Capital Budget 1990
British Columbia Rapid Transit Company	33,500	$25,800
Calgary Transit	31,200	$25,483
Edmonton Transit	7,000	$27,000
Government of Ontario Transit	24,820	$266,473
Montreal Urban Community Transit Corporation	216,428	$5,600
Toronto Transit Commission	384.9	$76,504

* All figures in thousands (add 000)
  Canadian figures in Canadian dollars

Total Operating Budget 1990	Total Capital Requirements Next 10yrs	Total Operating Requirements Next 10yrs	Federal Subsidy Requirements Next 10yrs
—	$383,000	$47,000	$0
$23,904	$37,754	$298,449	$48,929
$133,000	$720,000	$2,500,000	$0
$21,754	$131,125	$331,155	$99,450
$8,100	$579,000	$803,300	$498,514
$14,000	$1,325,000	$250,000	$933,750
$186,836	$3,254,064	$2,777,800	$1,149,554
$69,095	$951,200	$1,182,900	$751,253
$17,144	$1,806,200	$361,655	$1,042,890
$219,726	$3,623,000	$3,307,674	$3,806,000
$40,000	$8,864,000	$2,136,000	$6,230,000
$16,833	$232,800	$295,849	$113,400
$6,869	$1,043,733	$122,763	$835,719
$11,000	$91,950	$148,500	$100,963
$234,978	$3,481,660	$3,712,000	$2,588,671
$2,536	$2,300	$29,680	$0

Total Operating Budget 1990	Total Capital Requirements Next 10yrs	Total Operating Requirements Next 10yrs	Provincial Subsidy Requirements Next 10yr s
$29,745	$1,221,500	$477,840	$1,155,045
$20,952	$329,548	$288,509	$312,851
$9,200	$275,000	$140,000	$214,650
$73,569	$2,468,048	—	$2,468,048
$301,000	$550,000	$3,895,000	$284,000
$285,728	$8,521,400	—	—

Metropolitan Atlanta Rapid Transit Authority's rapid rail car on the East Line at Decatur Station

NORTH AMERICAN RAIL TRANSIT

U.S. RAIL SYSTEMS

National Railroad Passenger Corporation (Amtrak)

The National Railroad Passenger Corporation, better known as Amtrak, was created by the Rail Passenger Service Act, enacted and signed into law in October 1970. Formed to relieve the nation's private railroads from the financial burden of providing unprofitable intercity passenger train service, Amtrak was mandated to operate as though it were a profit-making entity and to use innovative marketing and operating concepts to fully develop the potential of modern rail passenger service to meet the nation's transportation needs.

When Amtrak began operations on May 1, 1971, it had no employees, no trackage, no stations or maintenance facilities. It had inherited a dilapidated fleet of aging passenger cars and locomotives and depended on the freight railroads to operate the trains under contract. Today, Amtrak owns and operates more than 700 route miles, mostly in the Washington-Boston Northeast Corridor, and continues to operate over 23,000 route miles owned and maintained by the freight railroads. Amtrak's intercity trains serve more than 500 destinations in 44 states.

By improving service, aggressively marketing its products, improving productivity and controlling costs, Amtrak revenues have grown more than $1.3 billion annually, covering 80% of its operating costs. Amtrak expects to cover all operating costs and eliminate the need for federal operating support by the year 2000.

Although created as an intercity carrier, Amtrak has become an operator of commuter rail services under contract to local transit authorities. It began operating Baltimore-Washington commuter trains for Maryland DOT in 1983; all Boston area commuter rail services for Massachusetts Bay Transit Authority in 1987; Shore Line East commuter service for Connecticut DOT in 1990; and Orange County, California commuter service in 1990.

Amtrak aggressively pursues other opportunities to operate contract commuter services as well as high-speed rail service.

National Railroad Passenger Corporation (AMTRAK)

	1985	1990	2000	*Projected 10-Year Total	Comments
Rail Ridership	20,777	22,187			
Rail Agency Employees (Include Administrative Support)	20,270	23,330			
Track Miles	24,000	24,000	25,500		Amtrak owns about 700 route miles in the Northeast, Michigan and New York. Elsewhere it operates over lines owned by freight railroads.
Number of Rail Vehicles (All Types): In Operation	2,145	2,301			
Refurbished					
Replaced					
**Annual Capital Budget (Rail Only)	$112,800	$202,700	$600,000	$5,400,000	Financial projections estimated by APTA based on data from Batelle Institute.
**Annual Operating Budget (Rail Only)	$1,600,100	$2,011,800	$2,695,812	$11,769,030	
**Total Rail Budget	$1,712,900	$2,214,500	$3,295,812	$17,169,030	
**Portion of Rail Budget Paid With Federal Funds if Available (Based on Current Law): Capital	$52,300	$83,600	$240,000	$2,160,000	
Operating	$627,000	$521,100	$0	$1,471,129	Amtrak plans to phase out operating assistance by FY 2000.
Total	$679,300	$604,700	$240,000	$3,631,129	

Governing Board: National Railroad Passenger Corporation Board of Directors
60 Massachusetts Avenue, N. E.
Washington, D. C. 20002
Telephone: (202) 906-3000   Telefax: (202) 906-2949

Chair: W. Graham Claytor, Jr.
Members: Haley Barbour, Eugene Croisant, David F. Girard-diCarlo, Charles Luna, Samuel Skinner, Governor Tommy Thompson, Carl W. Vogt, Paul M. Weyrich

President: W. Graham Claytor, Jr.
60 Massachusetts Avenue, N. E.
Washington, D. C. 20002
Telephone: (202) 906-3000

Purchasing Agent: Floyd L. Kemerer, Assistant Vice President, Materials Management
30th Street Station
Philadelphia, Pennsylvania 19104
Telephone: (215) 349-1190

Sum of Annual figures for 1991-2000.   ** Ridership and financial figures in thousands.

California Department of Transportaton (Peninsula Commute Service)

The Peninsula Commute Service or "CalTrain" is 47 miles long, extending from San Francisco to San Jose. It is operated for the California Department of Transportation (Caltrans) by the Southern Pacific Transportation Company (SP).

On weekdays 54 trains are operated (27 in each direction) between San Francisco and San Jose. Approximately two-thirds of these trains are concentrated within the morning and evening peak periods. All-day weekend service is provided with 26 trains (13 in each direction) on Saturday, and 20 trains (ten in each direction) on Sunday. There is also a midnight departure from San Francisco on Fridays and Saturdays.

Trains are also operated for special events, such as the "Bay to Breakers" race in San Francisco and the "Big Game" held at Stanford University. Special trains are chartered for events such as the Martin Luther King, Jr. Birthday celebration in San Francisco in January and the Gilroy Garlic Festival in July.

There are 26 stations served by CalTrain, and two additional stops (Stanford and Bay Meadows) are made for football and horse racing events. Seven of the stations are historic properties that have been restored.

Weekday ridership is approximately 22,000. Fares vary with the distance traveled between six zones. A one-way ticket for travel between San Jose and San Francisco costs $3.50, but a variety of discount fares is available. Tickets are sold at 11 stations, and can also be purchased aboard trains. It takes about one hour and 25 minutes to travel the entire 47-mile route, but express service is provided during commute peak periods which reduces total travel time to slightly over one hour.

CALIFORNIA DEPARTMENT OF TRANSPORTATION (CALTRANS)

	1985	1990	2000	*Projected 9-Year Total°	Comments
**Rail Ridership	5,300	6,400	10,000	71,000	°Figures reflect FY 1990-1999 only
Rail Agency Employees (Include Administrative Support)	370[1]	368[1]	370[1]		[1]Southern Pacific contract employees
Track Miles	46.9 DT	46.9 DT	19.0 ST 55.9 DT		DT = Double track ST = Single track
Number of Rail Vehicles (All Types): In Operation		93	140		
Refurbished	0	0	0	20	Locomotive overhaul
Replaced	93	0	0	0	
**Annual Capital Budget (Rail Only)	$9,400	$32,131	$11,994	$1,377,270	Capital Plan goes through FY 1996-97 only. Major capital expansions planned in 1991 and 1996.
**Annual Operating Budget (Rail Only)	$24,837	$28,561	$30,000	$300,000	
**Total Rail Budget	$34,237	$60,692	$41,994	$1,677,270	
**Portion of Rail Budget Paid With Federal Funds if Available (Based on Current Law): Capital	$4,500	$21,029	$8,998	$433,190[2]	Financing sources have no breakdown after 1993-94. [2]Right of way purchase excluded.
Operating	$2,000	$1,147	$1,200	$10,000	
Total	$6,500	$22,176	$10,198	$443,190	

Governing Board: The CalTrain system is the only passenger rail system directly run by the California Department of Transportation. It is currently run by Acting Director A. A. Pierce and District 4 Director Preston Kelley.

General Manager:

George E. Gray, Deputy District Director
Planning and Public Transportation
California Department of Transportation
P. O. Box 7310
San Francisco, California 94120
Telephone: (415) 923-4286
Telefax: (415) 923-4299

John E. Grother, Manager
Joint Facilities
Southern Pacific Transportation Co.
One Market Plaza
San Francisco, California 94105
Telephone: (415) 541-1245

Purchasing Agent:

Jeffrey Abraham, Chief
Financial Management Section
California Department of Transportation, Rail Service Branch
Post Office Box 7310
San Francisco, California 94120
Telephone: (415) 557-8253   Telefax: (415) 557-4137

Los Angeles County Transportation Commission

Created by the California Legislature in 1976, the Los Angeles County Transportatic Commission (LACTC) is the principal transportation authority in Los Angeles County. LACTC's subsidiary, the Rail Construction Corporation, was created in 1989 to manage design and construction of the Los Angeles METRO Rail System.

Two half-cent sales taxes now provide over $800 million a year for public transit in Los Angeles County. The LACTC is designing an integrated transportation network callec the METRO system that will be implemented over the next thirty years. Coordinating the rail, bus, and highway networks, the METRO includes a broad mix of transportation mode and solutions. The rail transit system alone will consist of more than 300 miles of light rai heavy rail (subways) and commuter rail by 2010, carrying a total daily passenger load expected to exceed 500,000.

The first completed link in the rail system, a 22-mile light rail line between downtow Long Beach and downtown Los Angeles called the METRO Blue Line, opened July 14, 1990. The METRO Red Line, an 18-mile underground heavy rail system that will serve th core of Los Angeles County, is under construction with the first phase due for completion i September 1993. Also under construction is the METRO Green Line, which will be the nation's first fully automated rail rapid transit. Running between Norwalk and El Segundo down the middle of the Glenn Anderson (I-105) Freeway, this line will offer computer-operated, driverless trains to more than 25,000 daily riders when it opens in 1994. Rail projects are being developed in other corridors as well. The LACTC has planned routes fo an east-west rail line in the San Fernando Valley and for a line from downtown Los Angele to Pasadena.

The LACTC is working to develop commuter rail lines in cooperation with its five neighboring counties. Using existing rights-of-way, commuter rail service connecting Los Angeles with Simi Valley, Santa Clarita Valley, and San Bernardino is expected to be operational by 1992. Commuter rail service into Riverside and Orange Counties is plannec for the near future.

LOS ANGELES COUNTY TRANSPORTATION COMMISSION (LACTC)

	1985	1990	2000	*Projected 10-Year Total	Comments
**Rail Ridership	—	—	94,200	378,300	Projections include Long Beach-Los Angeles Blue Line, Pasadena Line, Glendale Line, Red Line subway system (all 3 phases) and Valley leg of subway line, Green Line
Rail Agency Employees (Include Administrative Support)	—	—	$5,000^0$		
Track Miles	—	—	99^1		
Number of Rail Vehicles (All Types): In Operation	—	—	374^2		LACTC's light rail system is operated by the Southern California Rapid Transit District. LACTC and RTD data have been combined in U.S. Mass Transit Needs Summary Table.
Refurbished	—	—	50	50	
Replaced	—	—	0	0	
**Annual Capital Budget (Rail Only)	—	—	$834,000	$12,053,000	^{0}Includes contract and overhead employees
**Annual Operating Budget (Rail Only)	—	—	$310,000	$1,395,000	^{1}Double track; 55.7 commuter rail
**Total Rail Budget	—	—	$1,144,000	$14,448,000	^{2}107 commuter rail
**Portion of Rail Budget Paid With Federal Funds if Available (Based on Current Law): Capital	—	—	$363,000	$8,475,000	
Operating	—	—	$28,500	$125,000	
Total	—	—	$391,500	$8,600,000	

Governing Board: **Los Angeles County Transportation Commission**
818 West Seventh Street, Suite 1100
Los Angeles, California 90017
Telephone: (213) 623-1194   Telefax: (213) 244-6010

Chair: Councilman Ray Grabinski
Members: Supervisor Michael D. Antonovich, Vice Chair; Councilman Richard Alatorre; Mayor Pro Tem Jacki Bachrach; Ex Officio representing State of California Jerry B. Baxter; Mayor Tom Bradley; Supervisor Deane Dana; Supervisor Edmund D. Edelman; Supervisor Kenneth Hahn; Councilwoman Judith Hathaway-Francis; Supervisor Gloria Molina; James L. Tolbert

Rail Construction Corporation (RCC is a subsidiary of LACTC)
Chair: Ernest M. Camacho
Members: Robert E. Kruse, Vice Chair; David E. Anderson; Dr. Herbert L. Carter; Judith L. Hopkinson; Donald F. McIntyre; James T. Pott

Executive Director: Neil Peterson
818 West Seventh Street, Suite 1100
Los Angeles, California 90017
Telephone: (213) 623-1194   Telefax: (213) 244-6010

Purchasing Agent: Dilva Andrews, General Services Coordinator
Telephone: (213) 244-6585   Telefax: (213) 244-6005

* Sum of Annual figures for 1991-2000.   ** Ridership and financial figures in thousands.

North San Diego County Transit Development Board

San Diego County was connected to the rest of the nation by the California Southern Railway in 1884. In 1887 direct service to Los Angeles began. Since that time, numerous daily passenger trains have provided quick and convenient service between San Diego, Orange County and the Los Angeles Basin.

In 1987 the voters of San Diego County approved a 1/2-cent sales tax for specific transportation improvements. The list of programs funded included $70 million for Oceanside to San Diego commuter rail and $60 million for a light rail line between Oceanside and Escondido.

The North San Diego County Transit Development Board, a state-created transit agency, is to be the lead agency on both projects. NSDCTDB is currently exploring methods of gaining access to the right of way for these projects. Once access has been arranged the Oceanside to San Diego commuter rail service should start within three years and Oceanside to Escondido light rail service should start within seven years

NSDCTDB is additionally working with Caltrans, the Los Angeles-San Diego Rail Corridor Agency, the Orange County Transportation Commission and the Southern California Regional Rail Authority to improve the intercity service on the LOSSAN Corridor and implement commuter rail service north from Oceanside into Orange County and the Los Angeles Basin.

North San Diego County Transit Development Board (NSDCTDB)

	1985	1990	2000	*Projected 10-Year Total	Comments
1. **Rail Ridership	—	—	1,898	13,140	Oceanside-San Diego only.
2. *Rail Agency Employees* (Include Administrative Support)	—	2	38		Estimated figures for Oceanside-San Diego only. No figures available for Oceanside-Escondido, as planning is in preliminary stages.
3. *Track Miles*	—	—	64°		°Single track
4. *Number of Rail Vehicles* (All Types): In Operation	—	—	50		
Refurbished	—	—	0	0	
Replaced	—	—	0	0	
5. **Annual Capital Budget* (Rail Only)	—	—	$38,300	$383,000	Capital budget projections include both Oceanside-San Diego and Oceanside-Escondido Lines. Operating costs and operator figures are estimates only and reflect numbers for Oceanside-San Diego from 1993-2000.
6. **Annual Operating Budget* (Rail Only)	—	—	$8,000	$47,000	
7. **Total Rail Budget*	—	—	$46,300	$430,000	
8. **Portion of Rail Budget Paid With Federal Funds if Available* (Based on Current Law): Capital	—	—	$0	$0	No federal capital or operating assistance is being sought. Project will use State and local funds only.
Operating	—	—	$0	$0	
Total	—	—	$0	$0	

Governing Board: **North San Diego County Transit Development Board**
311 S. Tremont Street
Oceanside, California 92054
Telephone: (619) 967-2828   Telefax: (619) 967-0941

Chair: Ann Kulchin
Members: Melba Bishop, John MacDonald, Kris Murphy, Celine Olson, Pam Slater, F. H. "Corky" Smith, Nancy Wade, Jacqueline Winterer

General Manager: Richard L. Fifer
311 S. Tremont Street
Oceanside, California 92054
Telephone: (619) 967-2828   Telefax: (619) 967-0941

Purchasing Agent: Ramona Peworski
311 S. Tremont Street
Oceanside, California 92054
Telephone: (619) 967-2828   Telefax: (619) 967-0941

* Sum of Annual figures for 1991-2000.   ** Ridership and financial figures in thousands.

Sacramento Regional Transit District

Electric rail transit service began in Sacramento in 1890. At the turn of the century streetcars in Sacramento were operated by three different agencies, two of which also operated fast interurban service to Stockton, Chico and San Francisco. The interurban systems fell victim to the automobile just prior to World War II, while the local streetcar system continued to operate until January 1947. In 1973 the State Legislature created the Sacramento Regional Transit District and charged it with the operation of public transit service in the urban area.

In the late 1970s a Citizens' Advocacy Group promoted the idea of a light rail transit system as a solution to Sacramento's growing transportation and air pollution problem. A combination of federal interstate transfer funds, state monies and local dollars were combined to design, construct and operate an 18.3-mile light rail system. Construction started in 1983 and the first leg of the system opened in March 1987. The balance of the starter line was opened for revenue service in September 1987. Built at a cost of $176 million, Sacramento's RT METRO is the least expensive federally funded transit project in the United States.

In 1990 Sacramento Regional Transit District commissioned a systems planning stud to determine and prioritize additional light rail construction in the Sacramento area. This study, recently released in draft form, outlines several extensions and new lines to be built in the next twenty years. Included are an easterly extension to the City of Folsom, a northeastern extension into the City of Roseville in Placer County, and a new line to the rapidly growing south area using either the Union Pacific main line or an abandoned Southern Pacific branch line for right-of-way.

Regional Transit's Board of Directors will decide in the next few months how best to serve the citizens of Sacramento with light rail extensions and expanded bus service as Sacramento aggressively addresses its unprecedented growth and the resulting need to mov people efficiently while providing a clean, healthy environment.

	1985	1990	2000	*Projected 10-Year Total	Comments
**Rail Ridership	—	5,700	18,142	117,710	
Rail Agency Employees (Include Administrative Support)	—	128	444		
Track Miles	—	18.3	36.3		Route miles Double track
Number of Rail Vehicles (All Types): In Operation	—	26	174		
Refurbished	—	0	26	26	
Replaced	—	0	0	0	
**Annual Capital Budget (Rail Only)	—	$5,200	$173,200	$579,000	
**Annual Operating Budget (Rail Only)	—	$8,100	$129,300	$803,300	
**Total Rail Budget	—	$13,300	$302,500	$1,382,300	
**Portion of Rail Budget Paid With Federal Funds if Available (Based on Current Law): Capital	—	$1,300	$129,900	$434,250	
Operating	—	$648	$10,344	$64,264	
Total	—	$1,948	$140,244	$498,514	

Governing Board: Sacramento Regional Transit District
1400 29th Street
P. O. Box 2110
Sacramento, California 95812-2110
Telephone: (916) 321-2800   Telefax: (916) 444-2156

Chair: Supervisor Grantland Johnson
Members: Councilwoman Kim Mueller, Vice Chair; Supervisor Illa Collin; Councilwoman Lyla Ferris; William Mazza; Councilwoman Lynn Robie; Emily Vasquez

General Manager: Thomas G. Matoff
P. O. Box 2110
Sacramento, California 95812-2110
Telephone: (916) 321-2989   Telefax: (916) 444-2156

Purchasing Agent: Greg Arico, Purchasing & Materials Manager
P. O. Box 2110
Sacramento, California 95812-2110
Telephone: (916) 321-2920   Telefax: (916) 444-2342

Sum of Annual figures for 1991-2000.   ** Ridership and financial figures in thousands.

San Diego Metropolitan Transit Development Board

The Metropolitan Transit Development Board (MTDB) came into existence in 1976 with the task of determining whether a modern guideway transit system was feasible for San Diego. By 1981 MTDB opened its first light rail transit project, the South Line, ahead of schedule and under budget. This project and a second (a short East Line extension which opened in 1986) totaling 20 miles and including 30 LRVs, 16 stations and appropriate maintenance facilities, were funded solely by local and state monies. In 1989 MTDB's third LRT project, the 11.5-mile extension to the East Line, opened for service. It was built using local, state and federal funds. A fourth project, a one-mile extension to the East Line within Centre City San Diego, was completed in 1990 and relied upon local monies only.

San Diego's LRT system is operated by an MTDB subsidiary, San Diego Trolley, Inc. San Diego Trolley now carries more than 50,000 riders a day on the 16-mile South Line and 18-mile East Line. Fifteen-minute service (which has been standard since 1983) has now been improved to every 7 1/2 minutes during peak hours on the South Line. And within the next few years, as SDTI's current fleet of 71 light rail vehicles is increased through a new order of 75 vehicles, MTDB and SDTI expect to provide 7 1/2-minute peak period service on the East Line as well.

In addition to service improvements, MTDB has more rail projects in the planning and engineering stages. By the year 2010 seven more LRT projects should be completed. These projects are expected to be financed from local sources (primarily a local transportation sales tax approved in 1987) as well as state and federal monies. MTDB's projects, when added to rail projects now underway by our partner in the northern portion of the County — the North San Diego County Transit Development Board — would give the San Diego area at least a 90-mile LRT network and 43 miles of commuter rail service. All rail lines are enhanced by a coordinated system of feeder and parallel express, urban and local bus routes.

SAN DIEGO METROPOLITAN TRANSIT DEVELOPMENT BOARD (MTDB)

	1985	1990	2000	*Projected 10-Year Total	Comments
**Rail Ridership	6,000	15,500	51,600	305,800	
Rail Agency Employees (Include Administrative Support)	98	243	396		Assumes growth of 5% per year
Track Miles	15.9	33.4	70.9		Double track
Number of Rail Vehicles (All Types): In Operation	24	71	275		
Refurbished	0	0	0	0	
Replaced	0	0	0	0	
**Annual Capital Budget (Rail Only)	$17,500	$50,000	$20,000	$1,325,000	
**Annual Operating Budget (Rail Only)	$6,200	$14,000	$37,100	$250,000	
**Total Rail Budget	$23,700	$64,000	$57,100	$1,575,000	^{0}Assumes 75% match based on federal law. MTDB expects $5 million in capital assistance in the year 2000 and $323 million from 1991-2000.
**Portion of Rail Budget Paid With Federal Funds if Available (Based on Current Law): Capital	$9,500	$5,600	$15,000^0	$993,750^0	
Operating	$0	$0	$0	$0	MTDB federal operating assistance is applied to bus service.
Total	$9,500	$5,600	$15,000	$993,750	

Governing Board: San Diego Metropolitan Transit Development Board
1255 Imperial Avenue, Suite 1000
San Diego, California 92101-7490
Telephone: (619) 231-1466   Telefax: (619) 234-3407

Chair: Senator James R. Mills
Members: Supervisor Leon Williams, Vice Chair; Councilman Jim Bartell; Councilman Tom Behr; Councilman Dr. Robert Burns; Councilman Michael Dalla; Deputy Mayor Robert Emery; Councilman Bud Harbin; Mayor Mary Herron; Vice Mayor Jerri Lopez; Mayor Maureen O'Connor; Councilman H. Wes Pratt; Councilman Jerry Rindone; Councilman Ron Roberts; Mayor Joan Shoemaker

General Manager: Thomas F. Larwin
1255 Imperial Avenue, Suite 1000
San Diego, California 92101-7490
Telephone: (619) 231-1466   Telefax: (619) 234-3407

Purchasing Agent: Rick D. Thorpe, Director of Engineering & Construction
1255 Imperial Avenue, Suite 1000
San Diego, California 92101-7490
Telephone: (619) 231-1466   Telefax: (619) 234-3407

Sum of Annual figures for 1991-2000.   ** Ridership and financial figures in thousands.

San Francisco Bay Area Rapid Transit District (BART)

In 1947 a joint Army-Navy Review Board recommended that San Francisco and Oakland be linked by an underwater tunnel for high-speed electric trains. The State Legislature passed enabling legislation in 1957, creating the San Francisco Bay Area Rapid Transit District (BART). Engineering plans developed between 1957 and 1962 called for electric trains traveling 75 to 80 miles per hour in subways, at ground level and on elevated tracks.

BART officially opened on September 11, 1972 with eight two-car trains and service to 12 stations. Service to Richmond, Concord and through "the tube" followed within two years. The system-wide cost was $1.62 billion. The federal government paid 20%; the balance came from local and state sources, including bonds. Today BART is estimated to be worth $8 to $10 billion.

BART consists of some 2,650 staff and an elected nine-member Board of Directors operating 71.5 miles of dual track and approximately 450 cars between 4:00 a.m. and midnight each weekday, and 6:00 a.m. to midnight on weekends. It carries a quarter-million people to work and shopping every weekday, and nearly another 200,000 each weekend. After the October 1989 Loma Prieta earthquake, when BART was the backbone of cross-Bay and urban-suburban transportation in the Bay Area, the system carried more than 340,000 passengers each weekday.

By the year 2000, BART is planning to add 33 miles of double track and 10 stations to expand further east and south into the suburbs and to San Francisco International Airport. More than 10,000 patron parking spaces will be added.

As BART sits on the threshold of its third decade of operation, it is evident that the dreams and visions stretching back to the 1940s, coupled with the hard work of the '60s and '70s, created the first truly modern, high-technology urban transit system in the world.

SAN FRANCISCO BAY AREA RAPID TRANSIT DISTRICT (BART)

	1985	1990	2000	*Projected 10-Year Total	Comments
. **Rail Ridership**	65,458	74,761	85,897	780,796	Reflects Phase 1 extensions and four fare increases
. Rail Agency Employees (Include Administrative Support)	1,862	2,159	3,393		
. Track Miles	71.5	71.5	104.5[0]		Double track. [0] Reflects Phase 1 extension to West Pittsburg, Dublin, Colma, and Warm Springs.
. Number of Rail Vehicles (All Types): In Operation	439	589	713[1]		
Refurbished	0	0	0	439	[1] Includes purchase of 124 new vehicles for extensions.
Replaced	0	0	0	0	
. **Annual Capital Budget (Rail Only)	$56,058	$129,278	$73,420	$3,254,064	
. **Annual Operating Budget (Rail Only)	$140,437	$186,836	$386,200	$2,777,800	
. **Total Rail Budget	$196,495	$316,114	$459,620	$6,031,864	
. **Portion of Rail Budget Paid With Federal Funds if Available (Based on Current Law): Capital	$31,418	$26,814	$55,432	$1,149,554	BART is overmatching the federal capital funding formula intentionally due to expected federal funding shortfal. Federal operating subsidy to the region is expended on bus operations.
Operating	$0	$0	$0	$0	
Total	$31,418	$26,814	$55,432	$1,149,554	

<u>Governing Board:</u> **San Francisco Bay Area Rapid Transit District Board of Directors**
800 Madison Street
Oakland, California 94607
Telephone: (415) 464-6095   Telefax: (415) 464-6049

President: Erlene DeMarcus
Members: Michael Bernick, Vice President; Nello Bianco; James Fang; Joe Fitzpatrick; John Glenn; Sue Hone; Margret K. Pryor; Wilfred T. Ussery

<u>General Manager:</u> Frank J. Wilson
800 Madison Street
Oakland, California 94607
Telephone: (415) 464-6060   Telefax: (415) 464-6009

<u>Purchasing Agent:</u> William Thomas, Department Manager
Procurement
800 Madison Street
Oakland, California 94607
Telephone: (415) 464-6380

Sum of Annual figures for 1991-2000.   ** Ridership and financial figures in thousands.

San Francisco Municipal Railway

San Francisco has had transit service since 1852, when stagecoach-like vehicles called omnibuses began operating. Horsecar and steam train service started in 1860, and the world's first successful cable car service began in 1873.

Electric streetcars began operating in San Francisco in 1892. However, much of the cable car service was not replaced until the earthquake and fire of April 1906. Afterwards, most of the remaining cable car lines were on hills too steep for streetcars.

The Municipal Railway (Muni) began in December 1912, the first transit system to gain nationwide attention as a public service alternative to the private ownership which then predominated the transit industry.

The City acquired Muni's major competitor in 1944, and after World War II, most of the combined system's streetcar lines were converted to bus service, with much of the new service provided by electric trolley buses.

In the late 1970s and early 1980s, major route changes were implemented, and improvements were made to Muni's five remaining streetcar lines (now called Muni Metro), when new light rail vehicles were acquired and service began in the Market Street Subway.

Now, San Franciscans continue their strong financial support of Muni operations and improvements — over 45% of Muni's operating revenues come from the City's general fund, and in November 1989 city voters approved a 1/2-cent sales tax for transportation improvements. Improvements underway include extension of a Metro line and conversion of a diesel line to trolley-bus service. There are also plans for other Metro extensions and the implementation of historic streetcar service on Market Street and from The Embarcadero to Fisherman's Wharf.

	1985	1989	2000	*Projected 10-Year Total	Comments
**Rail Ridership	58,863	49,403	60,600	557,300	
Rail Agency Employees (Include Administrative Support)	1,060	1,021	1,159		Numbers include only MUNI employees, not those in support functions
Track Miles	61.6	64.2	77.2		Double track. Projections include MUNI Metro Turnback, MUNI Metro Extension, J-Connection, F-MARKET/ EMBARCADERO, and Metro East
Number of Rail Vehicles (All Types): In Operation	176	184	246		
Refurbished	0	0	4	60	
Replaced	0	0	0	128	
**Annual Capital Budget (Rail Only)	$1,000	$36,000	$90,000	$951,200	
**Annual Operating Budget (Rail Only)	$57,155	$69,095	$170,400	$1,182,900	
**Total Rail Budget	$58,155	$105,095	$260,400	$2,134,100	
**Portion of Rail Budget Paid With Federal Funds if Available (Based on Current Law): Capital	$500	$18,000	$67,500	$713,400	Capital subsidy projections assume 75% federal share based on current law.
Operating	$2,400	$2,211	$5,453	$37,853	
Total	$2,900	$20,211	$72,953	$751,253	

Governing Board: **San Francisco Public Utilities Commission**
City Hall, Room 287
San Francisco, California 94102
Telephone: (415) 554-7316   Telefax: (415) 554-7470

President: Sherri Chiesa
Members: Gordon Chin, Vice President; H. Welton Flynn; Arthur Toupin; vacant

General Manager: Johnny Stein
San Francisco Municipal Railway
949 Presidio Avenue
San Francisco, California 94115
Telephone: (415) 923-6212
Telefax: (415) 923-6218

Tom Elzey
San Francisco Public Utilites Commission
City Hall, Room 287
San Francisco, California 94102
Telephone: (415) 554-7316
Telefax: (415) 554-7470

Purchasing Agent: PUC Finance Bureau
Purchasing Department
425 Mason Street
San Francisco, California 94102
Telephone: (415) 923-2519   Telefax: (415) 923-3672

Santa Clara County Transportation Agency

Rail came to Santa Clara County along with the Transcontinental Railroad in the 1860s. Horse-drawn trolleys and steam engines evolved into 126 miles of trolley and interurban tracks which crisscrossed the Santa Clara Valley, interconnecting city centers and suburbs. In 1937 that fine system was purchased by National City Lines, put out of business, and replaced by bus service, except for the Southern Pacific commute connection to San Francisco.

In 1973 Santa Clara County residents voted to establish a Transit District, with the County Board of Supervisors as the Board of Directors. The Board is advised by a County Transportation Commission which includes at least one representative from each of the County's 15 cities.

In 1976 the public voted a 1/2-cent sales tax to build a rail system and renovate and expand the bus system. The alternatives analyses and environmental studies begun in 1973 resulted in the Guadalupe Corridor Light Rail Project which began construction in 1984 and began partial operation in 1988, with full operation on the 21-mile line beginning April 25, 1991. The $550 million project is funded 50% with federal funds and 50% with local and state funds.

"Transportation 2000," the County's current long-range master plan, includes three light rail extensions, a BART extension, and a CalTrain acquisition, extension and upgrade to be underway before the turn of the century. The county's all-important bus fleet will increase from 550 to 790 during that period. The update to that master plan, "Transportation 2010," envisions as many as nine additional light rail extensions, stretching the system to over 100 miles by 2010.

The ultimate system will have a classic commute loop with spokes interconnecting suburb cities and also providing access to major employers, universities and other trip generators. Santa Clara County, known as Silicon Valley, is rolling into the 21st century on rail!

SANTA CLARA COUNTY TRANSPORTATION AGENCY (SCCTA)

	1985	1990	2000	*Projected 10-Year Total	Comments
Rail Ridership	—	3,600	10,500	73,350	All projections include completion of Guadalupe, Tasman, Vasona, and Capitol LRT lines; construction of De Anza and Evergreen LRT lines and BART.
Rail Agency Employees (Include Administrative Support)	—	162	417		
Track Miles	—	9.2^0	46.4^0		°Double track
Number of Rail Vehicles (All Types): In Operation	—	14	119		
Refurbished	—	5	20	20	
Replaced	—	0	0	0	
**Annual Capital Budget (Rail Only)	—	$2,000	$440,000	$1,806,200	
**Annual Operating Budget (Rail Only)	—	$17,144	$57,460	$361,655	Includes CalTrain subsidy; Guadalupe, Tasman, Vasona and Capitol operations.
**Total Rail Budget	—	$19,144	$497,460	$2,167,855	
**Portion of Rail Budget Paid With Federal Funds if Available (Based on Current Law): Capital	—	$0	$307,500	$1,035,000	75% federal share for Tasman and De Anza LRT and BART line. Other projects locally funded.
Operating	—	$580	$998	$7,890	Escalated at 5%
Total	—	$580	$308,498	$1,042,890	

Governing Board: **Santa Clara County Transit District Board of Supervisors**
70 W. Hedding Street, 10th Floor
San Jose, California 95110
Telephone: (408) 299-2323   Telefax: (408) 298-8460

Chair: Supervisor Rod Diridon
Members: Supervisor Dianne McKenna, Vice Chair; Supervisor Ron Gonzales; Supervisor Michael M. Honda; Supervisor Zoe Lofgren

Director: Lawrence Reuter
P. O. Box 611900
San Jose, California 95161-1900
Telephone: (408) 299-2884   Telefax: (408) 275-6836

Purchasing Agent: Jerry Rosenquist, Deputy Director
Fiscal Resources
P.O. Box 611900
San Jose, California 95161-1900
Telephone: (408) 299-2884   Telefax: (408) 275-6836

Sum of Annual figures for 1991-2000.   ** Ridership and financial figures in thousands.

Southern California Rapid Transit District

Rail came to Los Angeles County in the late 19th century. In 1901 Henry E. Huntington transformed rail transportation when he created the Pacific Electric Company and launched a large-scale trolley expansion program designed to connect the "woods to the city." Prior to their demise in 1961, the "Red Cars" transported riders throughout a 1,164-mile rail system serving Los Angeles, San Bernardino, Riverside and Orange counties.

In the aftermath of World War II, the electric cars were replaced by competing bus lines that offered more freedom of movement in an era of decentralized growth.

In 1980 voters approved a 1/2-cent sales tax to improve transit, which is helping to pay for a new rail system now being constructed in increments. Ground breaking for L.A.'s Red Line subway was in 1986. Planning for the next segments of the Metro project continues.

Rail was resurrected in Los Angeles County with the birth of the 22-mile Long Beach to Los Angeles light rail system in July 1990, 29 years after the Red Cars ceased running. Full operation commenced in February 1991. The $900 million project was funded through federal, state and local dollars. More than 24,000 boarding passengers ride the Blue Line every day. The RTD Blue Line represents the first leg of a planned 300-mile, $7.5 billion rail network that eventually will span a five-county area.

In 1964 the California Legislature created the Southern California Rapid Transit District (SCRTD), a public agency with authority to exercise eminent domain and responsibility for operating bus and rapid transit rail systems to serve Los Angeles County. The District is governed by an 11-member Board of Directors.

SOUTHERN CALIFORNIA RAPID TRANSIT DISTRICT (SCRTD)

	1985	1990	2000	*Projected 10-Year Total	Comments
Rail Ridership	—	6,500	110,000	490,000	System began operation July 1990. All figures are projections.
Rail Agency Employees (Include Administrative Support)	—	515[0]	5,000		RTD operates rail lines built by LACTC. LACTC and RTD data have been combined in U.S. Mass
Track Miles[1]	—	22	300		Transit Needs Summary Table.
Number of Rail Vehicles (All Types): In Operation	—	54	600		[0]Includes Los Angeles County Sheriff's Department under
Refurbished	—	0	0	0	contract to provide security.
Replaced	—	0	0	0	[1]Double track
**Annual Capital Budget (Rail Only)	—	$350,000	$530,000	$8,864,000	Projections include Long Beach-Los Angeles Blue Line, Pasadena Line,
**Annual Operating Budget (Rail Only)	—	$40,000	$370,000	$2,136,000	Glendale Line, Red Line subway ststem (all 3 phases) and Valley leg of
**Total Rail Budget	—	$400,000	$900,000	$11,000,000	subway line, Green Line (Norwalk to El Segundo with North Coast
**Portion of Rail Budget Paid With Federal Funds if Available (Based on Current Law): Capital	—	$109,000	$397,500	$6,150,000	extension and 5 commuter rail lines)
Operating	—	$3,000	$11,000	$80,000	
Total	—	$112,000	$418,000	$6,230,000	

Governing Board: **Southern California Rapid Transit District Board of Directors**
425 S. Main Street, 2nd Floor
Los Angeles, California 90013
Telephone: (213) 972-4600   Telefax: (213) 972-4594

President: Marvin L. Holen
Members: Richard Alatorre, Vice President; Mas Fukai; Gerry Hertzberg; Don Knabe; Nick Patsaouras; Jay B. Price; Carl Raggio; Charles H. Storing; Gordana Swanson; James Tolbert

General Manager: Alan F. Pegg
425 S. Main Street, 6th Floor
Los Angeles, California 90013
Telephone: (213) 972-4310   Telefax: (213) 972-4325

Purchasing Agent: Paul Como, Director
Office of Contracts, Procurement and Materiel
470 Bauchet Street
Los Angeles, California 90012
Telephone: (213) 972-5150   Telefax: (213) 972-5053

Sum of Annual figures for 1991-2000.   ** Ridership and financial figures in thousands.

Denver Regional Transportation District

Although Denver once boasted over 150 miles of trolley lines and an annual ridership of over 36 million in the early 1900s, regular trolley service ended in 1950. Ridership on public transit fell to less than 60,000 annual passengers in 1971 due, in part, to the lack of a single region-wide provider. In 1969 the Colorado Legislature created the Regional Transportation District to formulate a plan for coordinated public transportation throughout the Denver region. In 1973 voters approved a 1/2-cent sales tax to finance a plan for a 98-mile network of personal rapid transit and an extensive bus system. In 1976 UMTA reversed its decision to fund the project, citing more pressing transit needs of other urban areas. Instead UMTA gave RTD significant federal money to upgrade the bus system. As a result, RTD purchased and consolidated the seven bus companies operating in the area into one coordinated agency.

In 1989 the Colorado Supreme Court ruled that RTD could collect a use tax on goods and services sold to persons living within the boundaries of RTD. This new revenue source was earmarked by the RTD Board for rapid transit. Enough money will be generated from this revenue source to construct a light rail "demonstration" project through the CBD, perpendicular to the successful 16th Street Transit Mall, using local funds without raising taxes.

Christened the Metro Area Connection, or MAC, the project will run for approximately three miles, connecting the Auraria Higher Education Campus, the CBD, and a burgeoning business center near the CBD. MAC headways will be five minutes during peak periods and ten minutes during off-peak periods. The system will run at grade on double track with contra flow operation in the CBD. Construction will start in early 1992 with opening day anticipated two years later.

	1985	1990	2000	*Projected 10-Year Total	Comments
**Rail Ridership	—	—	1,855	11,330	System scheduled to open to passengers in early 1994
Rail Agency Employees (Include Administrative Support)	—	—	45		
Track Miles	—	—	3		
Number of Rail Vehicles (All Types): In Operation	—	—	8		
Refurbished	—	—	0	0	
Replaced	—	—	0	0	
**Annual Capital Budget (Rail Only)	—	—	$0	$67,300	All financial figures in 1990 dollars
**Annual Operating Budget (Rail Only)	—	—	$2,436	$17,048	
**Total Rail Budget	—	—	$2,436	$84,348	
**Portion of Rail Budget Paid With Federal Funds if Available (Based on Current Law): Capital	—	—	$0	$0	Project will be built and operated with local funds
Operating	—	—	$0	$0	
Total	—	—	$0	$0	

Governing Board: Denver Regional Transportation District Board of Directors
1600 Blake Street
Denver, Colorado 80202
Telephone: (303) 299-2002   Telefax: (303) 299-2363

Chair: Jack McCroskey
Members: Glenda Swanson Lyle, First Vice Chair; Bernard L. Zimmer, Second Vice Chair; Cameron Winder, Treasurer; Michael J. Garcia; Dan Gray; Ken Hotard; Ben Klein; Steph Millard; Kevin Sampson; Roger Sherman; Tom Spooner; Helen W. Steele; George Stumpf; Bill Womack

General Manager: Peter Cipolla
1600 Blake Street
Denver, Colorado 80202
Telephone: (303) 299-2300   Telefax: (303) 299-2363

Purchasing Agent: Norman Levy, Director, Materials Management
1600 Blake Street
Denver, Colorado 80202
Telephone: (303) 299-2250   Telefax: (303) 299-2217

Sum of Annual figures for 1991-2000.   ** Ridership and financial figures in thousands.   53

Connecticut Department of Transportation

In 1969 the Connecticut General Assembly incorporated the Connecticut Transportation Authority (CTA) into the Connecticut Department of Transportation (CDOT). The Assembly authorized CDOT to jointly purchase and operate the bankrupt New Haven Railroad with the Metropolitan Transportation Authority of New York. CDOT provides approximately 60% of the operating deficit, 63% of the cost of movable capital assets. CDOT also provides 100% of the capital costs for projects in Connecticut.

In 1985 CDOT purchased the New Haven main line — a portion of the Northeast Corridor — running between New Haven and Greenwich including three branch lines (New Canaan, Danbury, and Waterbury). In 1989 CDOT purchased and upgraded New Haven shop and yard facilities, which became the base of operation for CDOT's commuter rail operations and will be completely rehabilitated by 1994. In 1990 CDOT instituted the Shore Line East service providing commuters residing east of New Haven with service to New Haven as well as connections to destinations west on Metro-North. The service is operated by Amtrak over a portion of the Northeast Corridor.

CDOT's "Statewide Transit System Plan" addresses Connecticut's transportation needs through the year 2010 and includes expansion and upgrade of the state's existing bus and rail systems. Of the more than $4 billion in transportation infrastructure projects identified in the plan, approximately $3 billion would be required for rail transit projects.

The primary goal of CDOT is to provide an integrated and balanced transportation system providing the state with the optimum level of service, choice, mobility, convenience and safety while having a positive influence on social, economic and environmental values. CDOT takes pride in its past efforts to meet this goal and continues to strive to meet the transit challenges of the present and future.

	1985	1990	2000	*Projected 10-Year Total	Comments
. **Rail Ridership**	14,266	16,309	22,259	195,815	All figures reflect implementation of Connecticut's Statewide Transit System Plan dated March 1991
. **Rail Agency Employees** (Include Administrative Support)	0	61	120		
. **Track Miles**	102	134	174		48 miles of 4-track, other is single track
. **Number of Rail Vehicles** (All Types): In Operation	179	228	382		
Refurbished	0	122	210	210	
Replaced	0	0	0	0	
. **Annual Capital Budget** (Rail Only)	$48,451	$58,217	$140,000	$1,856,600	
. **Annual Operating Budget** (Rail Only)	$108,524	$111,914	$196,036	$1,558,783	Assumes operating cost will be fully funded by State
. **Total Rail Budget**	$156,975	$170,131	$336,036	$3,415,383	
. **Portion of Rail Budget Paid With Federal Funds if Available** (Based on Current Law): Capital	$11,000	$10,125	$90,625	$1,392,000[0]	[0]Figure assumes 75% capital match per federal law. CDOT expects $180.6 million in UMTA capital assistance from 1991-2000.
Operating	$9,500	$9,041	$5,000	$55,000	
Total	$21,000	$19,166	$95,625	$1,447,000	

Governing Board: **Connecticut Department of Transportation**
Bureau of Public Transportation
P. O. Drawer A
Wethersfield, Connecticut 06129-0801

Commissioner: Emil H. Frankel
Telephone: (203) 566-3477   Telefax: (203) 566-4904
Deputy Commissioner: James F. Byrnes
Telephone: (203) 667-7300   Telefax: (203) 665-7204

Director of Rail Operations: Richard P. Rathbun
P. O. Drawer A
Wethersfield, Connecticut 06129-0801
Telephone: (203) 667-7364   Telefax: (203) 665-7204

Purchasing Agent: Benjamin P. Lenda, Assistant Director of Rail Operations (Support Services)
P. O. Drawer A
Wethersfield, Connecticut 06129-0801
Telephone: (203) 667-7338   Telefax: (203) 665-7204

Sum of Annual figures for 1991-2000.   ** Ridership and financial figures in thousands.

Jacksonville Transportation Authority

Jacksonville and the State of Florida became accessible to the more populous sections of the eastern United States when Henry B. Plant's organizing of all the small railroads serving northeast Florida resulted in through rail service into the city on January 10, 1888.

Horse-drawn trolleys were the only mode of public transportation in the town in the early 1800s. More than a half-dozen private companies competed until 1893 when the first electric trolley came into service. The first bus service was introduced in 1925, and in 1932 the electric trolley system was purchased by Motor Transit Company and route after route became part of the bus system.

In 1971 the Jacksonville Expressway Authority, created by the Florida Legislature in 1955 to build highways and bridges in Jacksonville, had its charter expanded to include operation of the City's mass transit system. This Authority was renamed the Jacksonville Transportation Authority, after the assets of the privately owned bus company were purchased.

Buses provided the only means of public transportation in Jacksonville until 1989 when a .7-mile "starter line" of a 2.5-mile dual guideway, automated and elevated transit system opened for passenger service.

JTA began planning for the Skyway in the mid-1970s. Final design is nearly complete on the second leg of the system. The final phase will cross the St. Johns River on the new Acosta Bridge now under construction.

Nine stations will serve the Central Business District which is bisected by the river. The Skyway's 14 vehicles will depart the stations at two-minute intervals carrying as many as 92 persons per car, increasing downtown mobility. Up to 5,000 fringe area parking spaces are planned, reducing downtown traffic and pollution. JTA buses also will interface at each of the three Skyway terminals.

	1985	1990	2000	*Projected 10-Year Total	Comments
Rail Ridership	—	399	32,000	161,500	1990 is first year of operation.
Rail Agency Employees (Include Administrative Support)	—	N/A	N/A		
Track Miles	—	.7	2.5		Double track
Number of Rail Vehicles (All Types): In Operation	—	2	14		Includes 2 spares
Refurbished	—	0	0	0	
Replaced	—	0	0	0	
**Annual Capital Budget (Rail Only)	—	$8,432	N/A	$135,000	
**Annual Operating Budget (Rail Only)	—	$617	$2,500	$14,000	
**Total Rail Budget	—	$9,049	$2,500	$149,000	
**Portion of Rail Budget Paid With Federal Funds if Available (Based on Current Law): Capital	—	$6,324	N/A	$101,250	
Operating	—	N/A	$0	N/A	
Total	—	$6,324	$0	$101,250	

Governing Board: **Jacksonville Transportation Authority**
100 N. Myrtle Avenue
Jacksonville, Florida 32204
Telephone: (904) 630-3181   Telefax: (904) 630-3166

Chair: Earl B. Hadlow
Members: J. Charles Sawyer, Vice Chair; Isaiah Rumlin, Secretary;
Ernest N. Brodsky; Richard M. Catlett; R. G. Greene; Bryan Simpson, Jr.

Executive Director: Miles N. Francis, Jr.
100 N. Myrtle Avenue
Jacksonville, Florida 32204
Telephone: (904) 630-3181   Telefax: (904) 630-3166

Purchasing Agent: Ervin A. Lovett, Jr., Deputy Executive Director, CFO
100 N. Myrtle Avenue
Jacksonville, Florida 32204
Telephone: (904) 630-3181   Telefax: (904) 630-3166

Sum of Annual figures for 1991-2000.   ** Ridership and financial figures in thousands.

Metro-Dade Transit Agency

The Metro-Dade Transit Agency (MDTA) is one of the largest departments of Metro politan Dade County Government. It is responsible for the planning and provision of all public transit in Dade County, Florida.

MDTA is a unified system which consists of four major components: Metrorail, the heavy rail rapid transit system stretching over 21 miles; Metromover, a double loop, 1.9-mile elevated people mover system that operates downtown; the Metrobus fleet which feed into both rail systems while also serving the remainder of the county; and Special Transpor tation Services, which provides transit service for Dade County's disabled residents.

The Metrorail system became a part of Dade County in 1979 when construction on the project first began. In May 1984 the system opened for service, and ridership and community support have been growing ever since. The electrically powered, elevated rail system extends over 21 miles from Dadeland, in the southern part of the county, through Hialeah which sits in the county's northwest section. The system has 21 stations along the line and connects a major portion of Dade County to a variety of cultural, business and shopping centers, as well as to Tri-Rail, the regional commuter train. Passengers can travel any distance for just $1.25 per boarding.

Metrorail can travel at speeds of up to 70 miles per hour, and travels the length of the system in just 42 minutes. There are 136 cars in the Metrorail fleet, each with a capacity fo roughly 150 passengers. Metrorail ridership is currently at over 50,000 boardings per day. Metrorail has service every 7.5 minutes during peak hours and every 20 minutes during off peak hours.

	1985	1990	2000	*Projected 10-Year Total	Comments
1. **Rail Ridership	4,857	13,622	29,671	200,821	The forecasts assume rail expansions of 12 miles in 1996, 1998 and 2000.
2. Rail Agency Employees (Include Administrative Support)	515	452	888		
3. Track Miles	50.7	53.2	89.2		Double track
4. Number of Rail Vehicles (All Types): In Operation	96	136	194		
Refurbished	0	0	0	0	
Replaced	0	0	0	0	
5. **Annual Capital Budget (Rail Only)	$90,604	$2,651	$250,049	$1,377,881	
6. **Annual Operating Budget (Rail Only)	$30,627	$43,632	$85,709	$608,644	
7. **Total Rail Budget	$121,231	$46,283	$335,758	$1,986,525	
8. **Portion of Rail Budget Paid With Federal Funds if Available (Based on Current Law): Capital	$0	$3,600	$55,585	$436,676	MDTA assumes no operating assistance for rail because the agency was already at the operating assistance cap for buses when the rail system was completed.
Operating	$0	$0	$0	$0	
Total	$0	$3,600	$55,585	$436,676	

Governing Board: **Metro-Dade Board of County Commissioners**
111 NW 1st Street
Miami, Florida 33128

Mayor: Stephen P. Clark

Transportation Committee
Chair: Charles Dusseau   Telephone: (305) 375-5117   Telefax: (305) 375-5569
Members: Alex Penelas, Harvey Ruvin, Arthur E. Teele, Jr.

Director: Chester E. Colby
Metro-Dade Center
111 NW 1st Street, Suite 911
Miami, Florida 33128
Telephone: (305) 375-5675   Telefax: (305) 375-4605

Purchasing Agent: Randall Kalember, Chief, Materials Management
Transit Procurement and Inventory Management
3401 NW 31st Street
Miami, Florida 33152
Telephone: (305) 638-7219   Telefax: (305) 638-0502

Sum of Annual figures for 1991-2000.   ** Ridership and financial figures in thousands.

Tri-County Commuter Rail Authority

The Tri-Rail system runs 67 miles from West Palm Beach south to Miami, connecting directly with Dade County's Metrorail. The concept behind Tri-Rail originated in 1985, when a tri-county subcommittee formed to study options for easing projected traffic congestion in the region recommended that a commuter rail line be established.

In 1986 the Tri-County Commuter Rail Organization (TCRO) was formed to begin building the system, giving way in 1989 to the Tri-County Commuter Rail Authority (TCRA). The TCRA's nine-member Board of Directors was designed to give control of the agency to local government.

The state of Florida purchased 81 miles of the CSXT corridor for $264 million and provided $59 million to improve the track, purchase rolling stock and build stations. The initial annual operating budget of $14 million was funded with four million from the Federal Highway Administration, eight million from Florida DOT and two million from Federal Oil Overcharge Funds. No UMTA funds were used during startup.

Tri-Rail started operating on January 9, 1989. Tri-Rail runs 20 bi-level daily trains during peak morning, midday and evening commuting hours, Monday through Friday. Saturday service began on December 8, 1991.

Tri-Rail's five-year Strategic Plan foresees the double-tracking of the corridor, purchase of more rolling stock, joint development projects and the addition of more parking. A direct connection into Miami International Airport and east-west connections between the airport and seaport in Miami have been recommended.

Tri-Rail now carries over 7,000 daily riders — an increase of 140% over ridership figures for January 1990. With a population of 4.2 million living in the tri-county area, the potential for Tri-Rail to gain additional riders remains promising.

	1985	1990	2000	*Projected 10-Year Total	Comments
Rail Ridership	—	1,419	N/A	N/A	
Rail Agency Employees (Include Administrative Support)	—	172°	N/A		°TCRA contracts for ticketing, security and train operations.
Track Miles	—	67	80		Single track
Number of Rail Vehicles (All Types): In Operation	—	23	45[1]		10 locomotives 35 passenger coaches
Refurbished	—	0	0	0	
Replaced	—	0	0	0	
**Annual Capital Budget (Rail Only)	—	$283,500[2]	$57,000	$232,800	Capital projects drawn from Strategic Plan. [2]Includes purchase of rail corridor, rolling stock and stations by Florida DOT.
**Annual Operating Budget (Rail Only)	—	$16,833	$36,600	$295,849	
**Total Rail Budget	—	$300,333	$93,400	$528,649	
**Portion of Rail Budget Paid With Federal Funds if Available (Based on Current Law): Capital	—	$200	$4,000	$90,000[3]	
Operating	—	$3,700	$2,000	$23,400	[3]$48 million in UMTA Section 3 funds, balance is Section 9 funds.
Total	—	$3,900	$6,000	$113,400	

Governing Board: The Tri-County Commuter Rail Authority was created by Florida State Statute to be an agency of the State. An independent Board of Directors is comprised of officials representing Dade, Broward and Palm Beach Counties.

Chair: Commissioner Carol A. Roberts
Members: Commissioner Ed Kennedy, Vice Chair; Ken Adams; Rick Chesser; Commissioner Charles Dusseau; Allen C. Harper; Terrance J. Mullin; Commissioner Lori Nance Parrish; David Rush

Executive Director: Gilbert M. Robert
305 South Andrews Avenue, Suite 200
Fort Lauderdale, Florida 33301
Telephone: (305) 728-8512   Telefax: (305) 763-1345

Purchasing Agent: John Boutwell, Director of Finance and Administration
305 South Andrews Avenue, Suite 200
Fort Lauderdale, Florida 33301
Telephone: (305) 728-8512   Telefax: (305) 763-1345

Sum of Annual figures for 1991-2000.   ** Ridership and financial figures in thousands.

Metropolitan Atlanta Rapid Transit Authority (MARTA)

Atlanta's growth has always been closely linked with transportation. And the city has been known as a transportation hub. In the 1950s the region's political and business leaders teamed up with planners and proposed a rapid transit system. But it was not until June 30, 1979 that Atlanta ushered in the rapid rail age with the opening of MARTA's East Line.

Today MARTA operates a 32-mile rail system and 150 bus routes. In 1971 residents of Fulton and DeKalb counties voted to tax themselves to finance a comprehensive transit system. Soon after the passage of the referendum, armed with a one-cent sales-and-use tax dedicated to transit, MARTA purchased the privately owned Atlanta Transit System. Over the next ten years, MARTA transformed the bus system into one of the safest, cleanest and most affordable systems in the U.S.

MARTA began construction of the rapid rail system in 1975 and, in only four years, the system began revenue service. Since that time the system has grown in increments to the present 32-mile, 29-station network. Aside from the initial service, one of the major milestones in MARTA's development was the opening of a rail link to Hartsfield Atlanta International Airport. MARTA had the foresight to build the shell of the airport station concurrently with the new mid-field terminal. The finish work was completed in 1988 when the line reached the airport. Today MARTA has the most convenient rail-to-air connection anywhere in the world.

The Authority plans to build a 60-mile system with 45 stations. Currently several stations are under construction, with Doraville and Bankhead scheduled to open in 1992. Kensington and Indian Creek stations will follow in 1993 and three more — Buckhead, Medical Center and Dunwoody — are slated to begin revenue service in 1995. MARTA's 240 rail cars and 681 buses travel 45 million miles carrying close to 150 million passengers a year.

METROPOLITAN ATLANTA RAPID TRANSIT AUTHORITY (MARTA)

	1985	1990	2000	*Projected 10-Year Total	Comments
**Rail Ridership	57,688	68,947	120,210	905,090	
Rail Agency Employees (Include Administrative Support)	703	1,443	1,483		
Track Miles	26	32	49		Double track
Number of Rail Vehicles (All Types): In Operation	150	238	300		
Refurbished	0	0	20	190	Start mid-life overhaul at rate of 20 vehicles per year
Replaced	0	0	0	0	
**Annual Capital Budget (Rail Only)	$189,069	$94,818	$74,000	$867,909	
**Annual Operating Budget (Rail Only)	$27,263	$60,708	$142,395	$952,121	
**Total Rail Budget	$216,332	$155,526	$216,395	$1,820,030	
**Portion of Rail Budget Paid With Federal Funds if Available (Based on Current Law): Capital	$117,000	$52,159	$55,500	$650,932	
Operating	$4,173	$2,214	$2,901	$29,007	
Total	$121,173	$54,373	$58,401	$679939	

Governing Board: **Metropolitan Atlanta Rapid Transit Authority**
Office of the Board of Directors
2424 Piedmont Road, NE
Atlanta, Georgia 30324
Telephone (404) 848-5050   Telefax (404) 848-5225

Chair: Ryland N. McClendon
Members: J. Paul Wade, Vice Chair; Julia Mitchell, Treasurer; George H. Ivey, Jr., Secretary; Amos Beasley, Jr.; Charles R. Brown; Harold Buckley, Sr.; J. David Chesnut; Marcus E. Collins, Sr.; J. Ray Crawford, Jr.; John G. Glover, Jr.; Hugh S. Jordan; Dr. Joseph E. Lowery; Sam Massell; Hal Rives; Dr. Charles J. Sargent; William "Sonny" Walker

General Manager: Kenneth M. Gregor
2424 Piedmont Road, NE
Atlanta, Georgia 30324
Telephone (404) 848-5050   Telefax: (404) 848-5225

Purchasing Agent: Ronald Nawrocki, Director of Contracts and Procurements
2424 Piedmont Road, NE
Atlanta, Georgia 30324
Telephone (404) 848-5272   Telefax: (404) 848-4294

Sum of Annual figures for 1991-2000.   ** Ridership and financial figures in thousands.

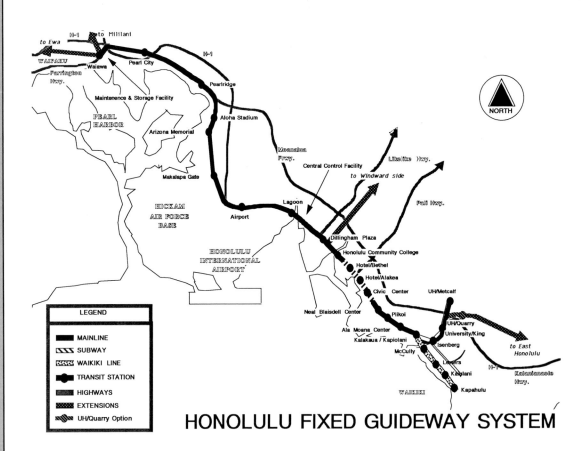

HONOLULU FIXED GUIDEWAY SYSTEM

Honolulu Department of Transportation Services

After almost 30 years of analyses and studies, the City and County of Honolulu is implementing an islandwide mass transportation system centered around a modern 17.3-mile fixed guideway rapid transit system with a fully integrated bus network. This integrated system will carry over 255,000 riders per day by the year 2005, providing sufficient capacity to meet Honolulu's mass transit requirements well into the 21st century.

The fixed guideway's western terminus will be in Waiawa and the double-track line will run to Waikiki and the University of Hawaii at Manoa on the eastern end. This line provides direct service to all of the major activity centers and destinations in Honolulu's densely populated urban corridor. The fixed guideway system will be a fully automated, electrically powered, grade separated medium capacity system.

The City has commenced the preliminary engineering phase of the fixed guideway project. In a concurrent effort the City will select a system contractor to design, supply, construct, operate and maintain the fixed guideway system using the specific automated rapid transit technology proposed by the system contractor.

The City expects to select the technology and award the contract in the late summer of 1991. Final design is expected to commence in mid-1992 with construction beginning in late 1992. Revenue service is expected to commence in 1997.

	1985	1990	2000	*Projected 10-Year Total	Comments
Rail Ridership	—	—	52,870	158,610	
Rail Agency Employees (Include Administrative Support)	—	—	200		
Track Miles	—	—	34.6		17.3 miles double track
Number of Rail Vehicles (All Types): In Operation	—	—	158		
Refurbished	—	—	0	0	
Replaced	—	—	0	0	
Annual Capital Budget (Rail Only)	—	—	$0	$1,241,000	All financial figures in 1988 dollars
Annual Operating Budget (Rail Only)	—	—	$35,200	$105,600	
Total Rail Budget	—	—	$35,200	$1,346,600	
Portion of Rail Budget Paid With Federal Funds if Available (Based on Current Law): Capital	—	—	$0	$930,750[0]	[0]Assumes 75% match based on federal law. Honolulu expects $372.3 million in UMTA capital assistance.
Operating	—	—	$3,600	$14,400	
Total	—	—	$3,600	$945,150	

Governing Board: **Department of Transportation Services, City and County of Honolulu**
The Director of the Department of Transportation Services reports to the Mayor of the City and County of Honolulu.

Director: Joseph M. Magaldi, Jr.
650 South King Street, Third Floor
Honolulu, Hawaii 96813
Telephone: (808) 523-4125   Telefax: (808) 523-4297

Purchasing Agent: Haruo Shigezawa, Purchasing Administrator
Department of Finance
530 South King Street
Honolulu, Hawaii 96813
Telephone: (808) 523-4867   Telefax: (808) 523-4847

Chicago Transit Authority

In 1859, when unheated horse-drawn streetcars operated, hay on the floors was used for insulation and kerosene lanterns were used for light. Today our gleaming stainless steel elevated cars criss-cross the city, moving a gigantic work force in hours, regardless of weather.

During 1882 cable car service began, followed in 1890 by the overhead trolley car. The latter replaced the horse-drawn streetcars and the cable car by 1906. Electric streetcars became the forerunner of an extensive people-moving-people system in Metropolitan Chicago.

1914 saw all the separate transportation entities consolidated under the Chicago Surface Lines, thus becoming the largest surface system under single management in the nation. In 1927 gasoline buses were introduced, followed by electric trolley buses in 1930. In the 1950s, buses totally replaced streetcars. However, as history often repeats itself, a light rail system is now on the drawing board for downtown Chicago.

Elevated service, or the "high line" as it was known, started in 1892 with coal-burning engines under the operation of several different companies. Steam engines soon replaced coal burners, and by 1895 we had developed the first electrically operated system in the world. Our famous "loop" elevated track, from which our downtown area drew its name, was built in 1897 and has become a symbol of Chicago.

The Chicago Transit Authority became an operating entity in 1947 when it assumed the operation of the surface and elevated lines. Since 1947 the CTA has continually provided cost-effective and convenient 24-hour service to established areas —now the City of Chicago and 37 suburban areas. CTA has become an integral part of Chicago's economic base, as thousands of residents rely on our services for their daily transportation needs.

Providing courteous and reliable service to one of the nation's largest metropolitan areas is an ever-present challenge being met daily by CTA personnel.

	1985	1990	2000	*Projected 10-Year Total	Comments
**Rail Ridership	—	166,757	175,000	1,700,000[0]	[0]APTA Estimate
Rail Agency Employees (Include Administrative Support)	—	2,328	2,628		
Track Miles	—	216	225		Double Track
Number of Rail Vehicles (All Types): In Operation	—	1,221	1,234		
Refurbished	—	8	830	830	
Replaced	—	0	256	256	
**Annual Capital Budget (Rail Only)	—	$390,734	$603,650	$5,134,470	
**Annual Operating Budget (Rail Only)	—	$278,905	$460,000	$3,694,000	
**Total Rail Budget	—	$669,639	$1,063,650	$8,828,470	
**Portion of Rail Budget Paid With Federal Funds if Available (Based on Current Law): Capital	—	$70,366	$452,000	$3,850,000	
Operating	—	$14,943	$24,000	$197,000	
Total	—	$85,309	$476,000	$4,047,000	

Governing Board: Chicago Transit Authority
Merchandise Mart Plaza
P.O. Box 3555
Chicago, Illinois 60654
Telephone: (312) 664-7200   Telefax: (312) 661-0112

Chair: Clark Burrus
Members: James I. Charlton, Natalia Delgado, J. Douglas Donenfeld, Kim B. Fox, Arthur F. Hill, Jr., Milton Holzman

Executive Director: Alfred H. Savage
Merchandise Mart Plaza
P.O. Box 3555
Chicago, Illinois 60654
Telephone: (312) 664-7200   Telefax: (312) 661-0112

Purchasing Agent: Craig Lang, Purchasing Manager
Merchandise Mart Plaza
P.O. Box 3555
Chicago, Illinois 60654
Telephone: (312) 664-7200   Telefax: (312) 828-9865

Sum of Annual figures for 1991-2000.   ** Ridership and financial figures in thousands.

Metropolitan Rail (Metra)

"Metra" is a service mark for all commuter rail service in northeast Illinois; the word is a marketing device that helps establish a unified identity for what was once a disparate assortment of commuter services operated by distinctly different freight railroads. There are both diesel and electric multiple unit operations.

Metra trains provide approximately 273,000 daily passenger trips, serving not only the six counties of northeast Illinois, but also reaching into neighboring Indiana and Wisconsin. Trains operate over 520 route miles, with 448 in Illinois. Over 3600 weekly scheduled revenue trains serve 231 stations. The annual operating budget exceeds $380 million. Close to 60% of all operating costs are earned through the farebox; the balance is covered by a sales tax surcharge levied in areas served by rail. Federal operating assistance amounts to less than one percent of costs.

There are seven "districts" of the overall Metra system. Three are directly owned and operated by Metra's corporate entity, the Northeast Illinois Regional Commuter Rail Corporation: (1) the former Rock Island route to Joliet, (2) the former Illinois Central Gulf electric service, now known as "Metra/Electric" to the south suburbs, and (3) two routes of the former Milwaukee Road to Elgin and to Fox Lake. There are three services provided by freight railroads on their tracks under purchase-of-service contracts: (1) Metra/Burlington Northern to Aurora, (2) Metra/Norfolk Southern to Orland Park, and (3) three routes on Metra/Chicago & North Western to Geneva, Harvard, and Kenosha, Wisconsin. The seventh service, to South Bend, Indiana, is a shared-subsidy operation with the Northwest Indiana Commuter Transportation District. The busiest single station on this Indiana-owned railroad is in the Hegewisch neighborhood of Chicago.

Metra has enjoyed consistent ridership increases since 1984, a reflection of the constituency's reluctance to make routine, daily, work-related trips to and from Chicago by private automobile.

	1985	1990	2000	*Projected 10-Year Total	Comments
**Rail Ridership	64,000	72,000	80,000	760,000	
Rail Agency Employees (Include Administrative Support)	1,135 NIRC 2,082 Contr. 3,217 Total	2,025 NIRC 1,126 Contr. 3,151 Total	3,151 Total		NIRC = Northeast Illinois Railroad Corporation Contr. = Contract carrier
Track Miles	520	520	520		Double track route miles
Number of Rail Vehicles (All Types): In Operation	1,016	1,021	1,139		Locomotives, diesel and electric cars. 33 electric cars owned by N. Indiana Commuter Transit.
Refurbished	50	46	0	540	Locomotives, diesel and electric cars
Replaced	0	0	0	263	Locomotives and diesel cars
**Annual Capital Budget (Rail Only)	$101,600	$111,731	$180,000	$1,802,000	1991-2000 operating projections assume annual expense growth rate of 4.75%
**Annual Operating Budget (Rail Only)	$245,664	$315,126	$501,215	$4,103,763	
**Total Rail Budget	$347,264	$426,857	$681,215	$5,905,763	Excludes system expansion through 2000.
**Portion of Rail Budget Paid With Federal Funds if Available (Based on Current Law): Capital	$79,800	$57,426	$50,810	$508,100	
Operating	$4,791	$4,448	$4,448	$44,480	
Total	$84,591	$61,874	$55,258	$552,580	

Governing Board: **Metra Board of Directors**
547 W. Jackson Boulevard, 13th Floor
Chicago, Illinois 60661
Telephone: (312) 322-6970   Telefax: (312) 322-4264

Chair: Jeffrey R. Ladd
Members: Gerald L. Porter, Vice Chair; Lowell E. Anderson; Jonathan B. Gilbert; Dr. Stanley
J. Hallett; W. Warren Nugent; Donald A. Udstuen

Executive Director: Philip A. Pagano
547 W. Jackson Boulevard, 13th Floor
Chicago, Illinois 60661
Telephone: (312) 322-6979   Telefax: (312) 663-4253

Purchasing Agent: G. Richard Tidwell, Deputy Executive Director
547 W. Jackson Boulevard, 13th Floor
Chicago, Illinois 60661
Telephone: (312) 322-8990   Telefax: (312) 322-8986

Sum of Annual figures for 1991-2000.   ** Ridership and financial figures in thousands.

Northern Indiana Commuter Transportation District

The first decade of the twentieth century saw the creation of an ambitious network of electric interurban railways. The South Shore Line Rail Passenger Service of the Northern Indiana Commuter Transportation District (NICTD), operating between South Bend, Indiana and Chicago Illinois, is the last of this once vast network.

The South Shore's best years were during World War II, when ridership climbed to over six million annual passengers. Returning veterans, helped by the GI Bill, bought new homes in the suburbs and once again readily available and affordable automobiles helped these veterans drive from the suburbs to jobs in the city upon newly constructed highways.

The South Shore had difficulty competing against this new mobility and entered a long period of ridership decline. By 1976, faced with mounting losses and deteriorating equipment and facilities, the South Shore attempted totally discontinuing passenger service. The Indiana General Assembly responded to the problem by creating a program of operating and capital financial assistance and forming NICTD in 1977. This action, coupled with financing from four Indiana counties, the State of Illinois, and the federal government, saved the South Shore from extinction.

Passenger service remained in private ownership and operated under contract with NICTD. The railroad changed hands in 1984 in a highly leveraged purchase and five years later was bankrupt. NICTD purchased the passenger assets from the court-appointed trustee and in December 1989 began directly operating the service. In 1990 with grants from the State of Indiana and the federal government, NICTD purchased the track and right-of-way.

NORTHERN INDIANA COMMUTER TRANSPORTATION DISTRICT (NICTD)

	1985	1990	2000	*Projected 10-Year Total	Comments
Rail Ridership	2,951	3,475	3,931	36,957	NICTD owns majority of 84 miles right of way and operates passenger service. Private freight company leases tracks for freight service.
Rail Agency Employees (Include Administrative Support)	—	215	270		
Track Miles	87.8	87.8	87.8		22 miles double track 65.8 miles single track
Number of Rail Vehicles (All Types): In Operation	48	47[1]	58		[1]34 owned by NICTD
Refurbished	0	0	0	0	
Replaced	0	0	0	0	
**Annual Capital Budget (Rail Only)	—	$21,000	$6,500	$85,000	
**Annual Operating Budget (Rail Only)	—	$23,500	$36,000	$295,000	
**Total Rail Budget	—	$44,500	$42,500	$380,000	
**Portion of Rail Budget Paid With Federal Funds if Available (Based on Current Law): Capital	—	$17,000	$4,875[2]	$63,750[2]	[2]APTA estimate for 1991-2000
Operating	—	$2,100	$3,600	$28,500	
Total	—	$19,100	$8,475	$92,250	

Governing Board: **Northern Indiana Commuter Transportation District Board of Trustees**
33 East U.S. Highway 12
Chesterton, Indiana 46304
Telephone: (219) 926-5744

Chair: William Carmichael
Members: David Staples, Vice Chair; Henry Kintzele, Jr., Treasurer; Phillip Barkley, Secretary; Clifford Arnold; Richard Jasinski; Donald Mulligan; George M. Smerk; William Smith

General Manager: Gerald Hanas
33 East U.S. Highway 12
Chesterton, Indiana 46304
Telephone: (219) 926-5744   Telefax: (219) 929-4438

New Orleans Regional Transit Authority

The Regional Transit Authority of New Orleans operates the oldest continuously operating street railway in the world, the St. Charles line. Begun in 1835 by the New Orleans and Carrollton Railroad Company, it had a profound impact on the development of the city.

For almost a century the St. Charles line was a part of a 200-plus mile network of urban and interurban passenger rail lines that crisscrossed the area; however, after all the rail systems were consolidated under New Orleans Public Service, Inc. in the 1920s, the rail lines were abandoned one by one in favor of modern buses.

In 1979 the Louisiana Legislature established the Regional Transit Authority, and in 1983 the RTA took control of the transit system. It is controlled by an eight-member Board of Commissioners with representatives from New Orleans and an adjacent parish (county).

With support and financial commitment from the private sector, in 1988 the RTA began a rail renaissance with the opening of the Riverfront Streetcar Line. Far exceeding its projected ridership in the first year, the line was expanded in 1990. Further expansion is planned.

As part of an overall rail plan for the Greater New Orleans area, the RTA has prioritized development of specific lines to increase the mobility of its citizens. A light rail line from the airport to downtown, streetcar lines in the central business district and additional commuter lines from outlying areas are all part of the RTA's plan to build a future on the foundation of its legacy of passenger rail service.

	1985	1990	2000	*Projected 10-Year Total	Comments
**Rail Ridership	6,277	8,346	10,475	100,000	
Rail Agency Employees (Include Administrative Support)	63	84	168		
Track Miles	13.5	14.3	60		Double track
Number of Rail Vehicles (All Types): In Operation	35	41	60		
Refurbished	0	6	45	45	
Replaced	0	0	0	0	
**Annual Capital Budget (Rail Only)	$0	$47,000	$92,000	$299,000	
**Annual Operating Budget (Rail Only)	$3,990	$3,990	$5,990	$14,000	
**Total Rail Budget	$3,990	$50,990	$97,990	$313,000	
**Portion of Rail Budget Paid With Federal Funds if Available (Based on Current Law): Capital	$0	$35,000	$69,000	$224,250	
Operating	$314	$274	$274	$2,740	
Total	$314	$35,274	$69,274	$226,990	

Governing Board: **Regional Transit Authority Board of Commissioners**
101 Dauphine Street
New Orleans, Louisiana 70112
Telephone: (504) 569-2600   Telefax: (504) 569-2867

Chair: Kern Reese
Members: Dan Alfortish, Ellenese Brooks-Simms, Dennis A. DiMarco,
Thomas D. Lacour, John LeBourgeois

General Manager: Justin Augustine, III, General Manager   Wayne Dupre, Executive Director
101 Dauphine Street
New Orleans, Louisiana 70112
Telephone: (504) 569-2600   Telefax: (504) 569-2867

Purchasing Agent: Gene Wulfekuhler, Director of Procurement
101 Dauphine Street
New Orleans, Louisiana 70112
Telephone: (504) 569-2600   Telefax: (504) 569-2867

Sum of Annual figures for 1991-2000.   ** Ridership and financial figures in thousands.

Maryland Mass Transit Administration (MTA)

The Mass Transit Administration (MTA), an agency of the Maryland Department of Transportation, is dedicated to providing reliable, safe, efficient, clean and courteous service. Mass transit has been moving people throughout the Baltimore area for over a century. Transportation in Baltimore has progressed from horse-drawn streetcars of the 19th century to operation of what is today one of the nation's largest transit systems. The 1950s and 1960s saw the planning of Baltimore's first major downtown renewal project. As the city began redevelopment, MTA was preparing to launch a rapid transit system aimed at meeting the future transportation needs of the area.

Construction of the first section of the Baltimore Metro began in 1976. The eight-mile, $797 million project was funded by both the state and federal governments. Metro revenue service began on November 21, 1983. Its automated fare collection system, based on magnetic tickets, integrates the subway with MTA bus lines.

In mid-1987 MTA opened a six-mile, $178 million northwest extension of the Metro. This addition was constructed in the center of the newly built Northwest Expressway, I-795. The summer of 1989 brought with it the start of construction on a second Metro extension. This new addition will extend service to Johns Hopkins Hospital in east Baltimore and is scheduled to begin carrying passengers in late 1994.
Additionally, MTA is currently constructing the Central Light Rail Line, a 22.5-mile line funded completely with state and local money.

In the spring of 1991, Maryland Rail Commuter service (MARC) came under the direction of the MTA when the State Railroad Administration was merged with the transit agency. MARC train service serves two states and the District of Columbia. The railroad includes 37 stations and three lines: Brunswick, Camden and Penn. Currently, 186 miles of line are in service and approximately 17,000 passengers are carried daily. MARC ridership is growing at a rate of ten to 20% a year. New locomotives and push-pull commuter rail cars were placed in service on all three lines in late 1986. MARC station construction, land acquisition, upgrading and parking lot expansion programs continue on all lines.

MARYLAND MASS TRANSIT ADMINISTRATION (MTA)

	1985	1990	2000	*Projected 10-Year Total	Comments
**Rail Ridership	11,190	17,068	31,110	240,890	
Rail Agency Employees (Include Administrative Support)	376	477	736		
Track Miles	158	164	229		
Number of Rail Vehicles (All Types): In Operation	121	180	375		
Refurbished	49	52	152	100	
Replaced	0	0	50	50	
**Annual Capital Budget (Rail Only)	$58,055	$155,943	$72,527	$762,322	
**Annual Operating Budget (Rail Only)	$23,947	$40,491	$65,900	$578,370	
**Total Rail Budget	$82,002	$196,434	$138,427	$1,340,692	
**Portion of Rail Budget Paid With Federal Funds if Available (Based on Current Law): Capital	$46,686	$58,206	$27,390	$416,176	
Operating	$2,390	$1,853	$1,830	$18,300	
Total	$49,076	$60,059	$29,220	$434,476	

Governing Board: The MTA is an administration of the Maryland Department of Transportation. The department is headed by the Maryland Secretary of Transportation who reports directly to the Governor. There is no governing board. Policy passes from the Governor through the Secretary of Transportation. Budgets are approved by the Legislature as part of the state's annual budgeting process.

Administrator/ General Manager: Ronald J. Hartman
300 W. Lexington Street
Baltimore, Maryland 21201-3415
Telephone: (301) 333-3885   Telefax: (301) 333-3279

Purchasing Agent: David R. Taylor, Manager of Purchasing
300 W. Lexington Street
Baltimore, Maryland 21201-3415
Telephone: (301) 333-3520   Telefax: (301) 333-3279

Sum of Annual figures for 1991-2000.   ** Ridership and financial figures in thousands.

Massachusetts Bay Transportation Authority

MBTA is the oldest subway system in America. The present Authority was created by legislation in 1964, encompassing 78 cities and towns in a service district with a population of 2.6 million. In addition, the MBTA serves 50 communities outside the district.

The Authority serves nearly 680,000 customers every day, over 100,000 more than in 1982. That's a 26 percent increase during a period when many transit systems nationally lost riders.

Service is provided by over 2,200 vehicles on four subway lines; 159 bus and trackless trolley routes; 11 commuter rail lines; commuter boats; and The Ride service for customers with disabilities. The MTBA has 130 subway stations, 101 commuter rail stations, and 10,000 bus and trackless trolley stops.

In the early 1980s the MBTA was a system in disarray. Physical infrastructure was grossly deteriorated, and breakdowns and missed trips frequent. Poor service resulted in confidence in the system hitting an all-time low. 1991 finds a very different MBTA. Thanks to $3 billion in capital investment (funded half by the federal government) and the passage of significant Management Rights legislation, the nation's oldest subway system is now one of the best. Customer surveys show a 92 percent satisfaction with service.

The $3 billion capital investment since 1980 saw completion of the Red Line Extension with four new stations, relocation of the Orange Line with nine new stations, the purchase of hundreds of new buses, Green and Red Line trains, and the repair of miles of track and other basic systems and facilities. This investment, in addition to vastly improving service, created an estimated 5000 construction and related jobs per year.

MASSACHUSETTS BAY TRANSPORTATION AUTHORITY (MBTA)

	1985	1990	2000	*Projected 10-Year Total	Comments
**Rail Ridership	155,800	192,300	237,000	2,133,000	MBTA commuter rail service is now operated by Amtrak; employee data include 1100 Amtrak FTE's
Rail Agency Employees (Include Administrative Support)	3,500	4,038	4,500		
Track Miles	310	331	377		Double track
Number of Rail Vehicles (All Types): In Operation	738	996	1,287		Capital program estimates assume all potential projects through 2000. Cumulative capital costs for all capital program projects assumed to be budgeted equally 1991-2000.
Refurbished	74	0	53	589	
Replaced	0	0	24	232	
**Annual Capital Budget (Rail Only)	$249,600	$383,710	$846,147	$8,461,470	
**Annual Operating Budget (Rail Only)	$263,216	$353,246	$575,400	$4,665,240	
**Total Rail Budget	$512,816	$736,956	$1,421,547	$13,126,710	
**Portion of Rail Budget Paid With Federal Funds if Available (Based on Current Law): Capital	$104,637	$75,579	$634,610	$6,346,102	
Operating	$12,250	$12,040	$12,040	$120,400	
Total	$116,887	$87,619	$646,650	$6,466,502	

Governing Board: Massachusetts Bay Transportation Authority Board of Directors
10 Park Plaza, 3rd Floor
Boston, Massachusetts 02116
Telephone: (617) 722-5098   Telefax: (617) 722-6180

Chair: Secretary of Transportation Richard L. Taylor
Members: Domenic Bozzotto, Toye Brown, Michael Hogan, Mary Noonan, James Radley, Albert Shaw

Acting General Manager: James E. Rooney
10 Park Plaza, 3rd Floor
Boston, Massachusetts 02116
Telephone: (617) 722-5176   Telefax: (617) 722-6180

Purchasing Agent: Robert W. Pittman, Director of Materials
10 Park Plaza, 2nd Floor
Boston, Massachusetts 02116
Telephone: (617) 722-3290   Telefax: (617) 722-5368

Sum of Annual figures for 1991-2000.   ** Ridership and financial figures in thousands.

Detroit Department of Transportation

The Detroit Department of Transportation (DDOT) serves the City of Detroit and 25 suburban communities along 55 line-haul bus lines. Established in 1922 as a public urban carrier, it has evolved through the years to its present place as the largest transit system in Michigan, carrying approximately 83% of the region's bus passengers.

In addition to bus operations, DDOT owns and operates nine vintage trolley cars on a two-mile track in downtown Detroit. The first cars made their debut in 1976 following several years of planning and searching for the vehicles. The electric-powered cars were built in England, Germany, Portugal and the United States between 1895 and the 1920s. The fleet of trolleys features seven closed and two open-air trolleys. One of the open-air trolleys is a double-decker — the only one of its kind operating in the world.

Acquiring and refurbishing the trolleys has been a public and private partnership. The city of Detroit, the State of Michigan and farebox revenues now fund the operation of the trolleys.

The Civic Center Trolley was an economic development project related to convention and tourism promotion. These antique trolleys have proven themselves one of Detroit's most popular attractions to tourists and conventioneers. In addition to providing great enjoyment to residents, they have proven to be very effective in attracting visitors by being featured in promotional advertisements, slides, films, etc. They have rapidly taken on the status of a "symbol of Detroit" much as cable cars serve San Francisco's fame.

DETROIT DEPARTMENT OF TRANSPORTATION (DDOT)

	1985	1990	2000	*Projected 10-Year Total	Comments
**Rail Ridership	35.1	24.4	25.3	248[0]	[0]APTA estimate Frequent service suspensions 1985-90 due to CBD construction.
Rail Agency Employees[1] (Include Administrative Support)	12	12	12		[1]Maintenance and operations only.
Track Miles	2	2	2		Double track
Number of Rail Vehicles (All Types): In Operation	8	9	9		Antique cars of varied native city origins
Refurbished	0	0	0	0	
Replaced	0	0	0	0	
**Annual Capital Budget (Rail Only)	$0	$0	$500	$500	
**Annual Operating Budget (Rail Only)	$350	$350	$350	$3,500	
**Total Rail Budget	$350	$350	$850	$4,000	
**Portion of Rail Budget Paid With Federal Funds if Available (Based on Current Law): Capital	$0	$0	$0	$0	
Operating	$0	$0	$0	$0	Supported by state and local funding and limited corporated sponsorship
Total	$0	$0	$0	$0	

Governing Board: The Detroit Department of Transportation is a department of the City of Detroit. The Department Director reports directly to the Mayor, Coleman A. Young.

Acting Director: Christopher K. Walton
1301 E. Warren Avenue
Detroit, Michigan 48207
Telephone: (313) 833-7666   Telefax: (313) 833-5523

Purchasing Agent: Karmun Newby, Manager
Materials Management
1301 E. Warren Avenue
Detroit, Michigan 48207
Telephone: (313) 833-0262   Telefax: (313) 833-5523

Sum of Annual figures for 1991-2000.   ** Ridership and financial figures in thousands.

Harris Graphic Des

Bi-State Development Agency

The initial phase of Metro Link is an 18-mile light rail line from the Main Terminal at Lambert-St. Louis International Airport to East St. Louis through Downtown St. Louis City. The combination of Metro Link with the regional bus system will provide access to major employment centers as well as principal retail, office, recreational, educational and medical centers.

Metro Link will use existing railroad rights-of-way, structures and facilities. Included are the rail deck of the historic Eads Bridge, a downtown railroad tunnel, and nearly fourteen miles of continuous railroad trackage. Nearly all of this railroad property is abandoned, but will be revived for Metro Link.

Metro Link will have twenty stations: fifteen at street level, three in subway, and two on existing bridge structures. All stations will be high platform to provide convenient access to mobility impaired passengers. Fare collection will be handled through a self-service, proof-of-purchase system. Additionally, the system will have over two thousand park-and-ride spaces available along the route.

Passengers will ride aboard a fleet of 31 double-ended, articulated light rail vehicles. The vehicles will be maintained and stored on a 12-acre site located adjacent to the main line. A unique feature of this project is the participation of artists in the design of the Metro Link system. Through the Arts in Transit project, artists have worked alongside architects and engineers on the design of stations, signs, landscaping and every other element of the Metro Link network.

The capital cost to build the initial phase of Metro Link is $288 million, covering design, engineering and construction. Future extensions of Metro Link are currently being pursued. The Bi-State Development Agency is building Metro Link which will be part of the fully integrated regional transportation system upon completion.

	1985	1990	2000	*Projected 10-Year Total	Comments
**Rail Ridership	—	0	23,600	95,200	1st segment open July 1993, 1st extension open July 1997, 2nd extension January 2000
Rail Agency Employees (Include Administrative Support)	—	2	410		
Track Miles	—	0	112.73		Double track
Number of Rail Vehicles (All Types): In Operation	—	0	84		31 LRV's on 1st segment, 23 LRV's on 1st extension, 30 LRV's on 2nd extension
Refurbished	—	0	0	0	
Replaced	—	0	0	0	
**Annual Capital Budget (Rail Only)	—	$121,333	$0	$1,134,434	No major rehabilitation required yet
**Annual Operating Budget (Rail Only)	—	$0	$38,000	$109,300	7 years of 1st segment 3 years of 1st extension 1 year of 2nd extension
**Total Rail Budget	—	$121,333	$38,000	$1,243,734	
**Portion of Rail Budget Paid With Federal Funds if Available (Based on Current Law): Capital	—	$91,000	$0	$850,826	
Operating	—	$0	$10,305	$103,050	
Total	—	$91,000	$10,305	$953,876	

Sum of Annual figures for 1991-2000.   ** Ridership and financial figures in thousands.

New Jersey Transit Corporation

New Jersey has a long and fruitful history of railroad operations dating back to the granting of a charter to the Camden and Amboy Railroad and Transportation Company in 1830 for the operation of the State's first commercial railroad. Commuter railroad operations have been integral to New Jersey's development and growth. Today NJ TRANSIT Rail Operations transports nearly 85,000 commuters on a daily basis.

NJ TRANSIT Rail Operations was established January 1, 1983, pursuant to the Northeast Rail Service Act of 1981, to take over the operation of commuter rail service from Conrail and its private railroad predecessors - Penn Central, Erie-Lackawanna, and Central Railroad of New Jersey.

NJ TRANSIT Rail Operations operates 569 trains each weekday on eleven rail lines. Frequent service is provided to New York, Newark, Hoboken, Atlantic City, Trenton and other points in New Jersey. NJ TRANSIT also operates trains under contract to Metro North Commuter Railroad into the State of New York. NJ TRANSIT passengers connect with SEPTA, PATH, and Amtrak rail services to travel to other destinations in the Northeast.

NJ TRANSIT has spent over $1 billion to replace old rolling stock and to refurbish, rehabilitate and renovate the centuries-old rail infrastructure and facilities. NJ TRANSIT is among the leading commuter railroads in the United States, with new passenger coaches and locomotives and attractive passenger and employee facilities. Riders have been attracted to NJ TRANSIT's "NEW" commuter rail service, with a ridership increase of 31% from 1983 to 1990, despite a recent economic slowdown in New Jersey and New York City.

NJ TRANSIT now has under development, design and/or engineering, plans to integrate existing rail services so that a rider from any station on one line can go to any destination on the other ten lines. This program envisions an investment of several hundred million dollars of private and public funds to provide full mobility to the State of New Jersey's citizens by the year 2000.

	1985	1990	2000	*Projected 10-Year Total	Comments
**Rail Ridership	34,347	41,833	43,700	427,665°	°APTA estimate for 10-year total does not include Port Jervis and Pascack Valley. [1]For year 2000, employee increases due to service changes are estimated to be offset by productivity improvements. [2]Route miles. Includes leased and trackage rights mileage.
Rail Agency Employees (Include Administrative Support)	3,529	3,655	3,655[1]		
Track Miles [2]	410	464	476		
Number of Rail Vehicles (All Types): In Operation	729	765	952		
Refurbished	70	0	92	509	
Replaced	0	0	0	35	
**Annual Capital Budget (Rail Only)	$127,661	$183,558	$565,070	$3,866,670	
**Annual Operating Budget (Rail Only)	$203,400	$283,600	$511,400	$3,965,100	
**Total Rail Budget	$331,061	$467,158	$1,076,470	$7,831,770	
**Portion of Rail Budget Paid With Federal Funds if Available (Based on Current Law): Capital	$107,781	$87,367	$423,802[3]	$2,900,002	[3]APTA estimates. Subsidy projections assume constant level of federal assistance. Capital projections assume 75% federal match based on federal law.
Operating	$19,700	$17,870	$17,870[3]	$178,700	
Total	$127,481	$105,237	$441,672[3]	$3,078,702	

Governing Board: New Jersy Transit Corporation Board of Directors
P. O. Box 10009
Market Street and McCarter Highway
Newark, New Jersey 07101
Telephone: (201) 643-7400   Telefax: (201) 643-4275

Chair: Thomas Downs
Members: State Treasurer Doug Berman, Martin Brody, John Kellogg, Eva Lerner-Lamm, John McGoldrick, Carl VanHorn

Executive Director: Shirley A. DeLibero

General Manager: Joseph S. Crawford, Jr.
1160 Raymond Boulevard
Newark, New Jersey 07102
Telephone: (201) 468-8021   Telefax: (201) 468-8574

Purchasing Agent: Frank Hopper, Assistant Executive Director
P. O. Box 10009
Newark, New Jersey 07102
Telephone: (201) 643-4963   Telefax: (201) 643-7480

* Sum of Annual figures for 1991-2000.   ** Ridership and financial figures in thousands.

Port Authority Transit Corporation of Pennsylvania and New Jersey

Formed in 1968, the Port Authority Transit Corporation of Pennsylvania and New Jersey (PATCO) is the rail transit operating subsidiary corporation of the Delaware River Port Authority (DRPA). PATCO operates and maintains the 14.2-mile, fully grade-separated rail line between 16th and Locust Streets in Philadelphia and Lindenwold, New Jersey. The line includes 13 passenger stations, seven of which have a total of 12,500 park and-ride spaces.

In Philadelphia, PATCO stations connect with the Southeastern Pennsylvania Transportation Authority's (SEPTA) bus routes, Broad Street Subway, and Market-Frankford Elevated Line. In New Jersey, PATCO connects with AMTRAK and New Jersey Transit a the Atlantic City Rail Line station in Lindenwold, and with New Jersey Transit and private operator buses.

The maintenance facility and administrative offices are located in Lindenwold, New Jersey. The revenue fleet consists of 121 electrically self-propelled high-performance stainless steel rail cars. The cars operate from a 750-volt third rail system. Average weekday ridership was 41,260 in 1990. PATCO operates trains 24 hours per day, 365 days per year, with train frequencies ranging from two to four minutes in the rush periods to 40 minutes between midnight and 5:00 a.m.

In recent years DRPA and PATCO have benefited from UMTA's federal capital assistance program. Recent UMTA-funded capital projects include rehabilitation of seventeen 80-year-old railroad bridges, rehabilitation and improvements to six station parking lots, installation of reverse cab signaling and a new double interlocking, Transit Car Mid-Life Overhaul and Upgrade Program, and accessibility improvements for the disabled at the Woodcrest Station.

Since inception, PATCO has averaged an 85% operating ratio. The annual operating deficit is funded from excess revenues of DRPA derived from bridge tolls from four DRPA bridges connecting New Jersey and Pennsylvania.

PORT AUTHORITY TRANSIT CORPORATION OF PA & NJ (PATCO)

	1985	1990	2000	*Projected 10-Year Total	Comments
**Rail Ridership	10,230	11,405	15,400	132,750	
Rail Agency Employees (Include Administrative Support)	330	325	325		
Track Miles	14.2	14.2	14.2		Double track
Number of Rail Vehicles (All Types): In Operation	121	121	121		
Refurbished	11	42	79	121	
Replaced	0	0	0	0	
**Annual Capital Budget (Rail Only)	$5,700	$10,725	$15,500	$131,125	
**Annual Operating Budget (Rail Only)	$17,668	$21,754	$41,775	$331,155	
**Total Rail Budget	$23,368	$32,479	$57,275	$462,280	
**Portion of Rail Budget Paid With Federal Funds if Available (Based on Current Law): Capital	$4,259	$8,142	$11,700	$99,450	PATCO's operating deficit is funded from excess revenues of the DRPA which are derived from bridge tolls.
Operating	$0	$0	$0	$0	
Total	$4,259	$8,142	$11,700	$99,450	

Governing Board: **Port Authority Transit Corporation Board of Directors**
Benjamin Franklin Bridge Plaza
Camden, New Jersey 08101
Telephone: (215) 925-8780

Chair: Rev. Nicholas S. Rashford, S.J.
New Jersey Members: Peter S. Burke, Jr., Vice Chair; William K. Dickey; Joseph P. DiRenzo; Robert A. Innocenzi; John M. Kennedy; Howard L. Moon, Sr.; Mayor Teresa A. Porrini; H. Donald Stewart
Pennsylvania Members: State Treasurer Catherine Baker Knoll; Lucien E. Blackwell; G. Edward De Seve; Hon. Vincent J. Fumo; G. Davis Greene, Jr.; Auditor General Barbara Hafer; Hon. Max Pievsky

General Manager: Robert G. Schwab
Administrative Offices
Lindenwold, New Jersey 08021
Telephone: (609) 772-6924   Telefax: (609) 772-6957

Purchasing Agent: Bernard J. Krant, Manager, Purchasing & Materials
Administrative Offices
Lindenwold, New Jersey 08021
Telephone: (609) 772-6914   Telefax: (609) 772-6957

Sum of Annual figures for 1991-2000.   ** Ridership and financial figures in thousands.

Long Island Rail Road Company (LIRR)

The Long Island Rail Road is the busiest, most densely configured commuter railroad in the United States. Over 720 trains run every weekday carrying more than 72 million customers annually between Long Island and New York City. A subsidiary of the New York Metropolitan Transportation Authority, the 157-year-old LIRR has played a pivotal role in the development of Long Island over its long history. It is today adapting its nine-branch, 700-plus-mile system to serve new markets in a mature Island economy, which is increasingly less dependent on Manhattan-bound commuting.

The railroad has reached the final stages of a massive $2.1 billion rebuilding effort between 1982 and 1991. Through that effort LIRR has added important new shops and yards, extended electrified track, purchased 174 new electric cars, and brought LIRR's right-of-way up to a state of good repair. The new Hillside shops are the most technologically advanced passenger rail car maintenance facilities in the world. The final major project of the 1982-1991 program involves rebuilding LIRR's primary New York City terminal, Penn Station, at a cost of $198 million, increasing access points by 40% stationwide and improving information, mobility and atmosphere at America's busiest commuter rail facility.

LIRR and MTA are working on a third five-year capital program for 1992-1996, designed to continue infrastructural renewal and good repair. To stabilize ridership during difficult economic times, the LIRR is studying ways to attract customers to non-traditional services during off-peak hours, especially commuter service from New York City to Long Island, and travel between points on the Island.

The LIRR's primary goal for the 1990s is to improve service quality by increasing the efficiency of its operation, imposing the discipline of the core rail operation on all areas of the company. With financial constraints for all levels of government more challenging than ever, and with traffic congestion an ever-worsening drain on Long Island's quality of life, LIRR's role in the Island's economy must expand and diversify. This the platform from which LIRR is launching its service toward the next century.

	1985	1990	1996	*Projected 7-Year Total[0]	Comments
**Rail Ridership	75,929	72,359	74,349	521,493	[0]Because of economic conditions and impact on ridership, forecasts are not available beyond 1996.
Rail Agency Employees[1] (Include Administrative Support)	6,948[1]	6,807[1]	6,764[1]		[1]Average annual number of employees.
Track Miles	681.2	701.1	701.1		Single track route miles
Number of Rail Vehicles (All Types): In Operation	1,165	1,200	1,153		
Refurbished	196	166	166		
Replaced	0	0	185		
**Annual Capital Budget (Rail Only)	$219,682	$208,700[2]	$270,460[2]	$1,769,700	[2]Projection is 1/5 of 5-year program total
**Annual Operating Budget (Rail Only)	$515,900	$611,500	$806,000	$4,947,500[3]	[3]1992-96 budget forecast
**Total Rail Budget	$735,582	$820,200	$1,076,460	$6,717,200	
**Portion of Rail Budget Paid With Federal Funds if Available (Based on Current Law): Capital	$54,920	$52,175	$67,615	$442,425[4]	[4]Approximately 25% of capital total
Operating	$13,420	$14,647	$13,378	$80,284	Based on January 1991 MTA assumptions.
Total	$68,340	$66,822	$80,993	$522,709	

Governing Board: **Metropolitan Transportation Authority Board of Directors**
347 Madison Avenue, 7th Floor
New York, New York 10017
Telephone: (212) 878-7200   Telefax: (212) 878-7031

Chair: Peter E. Stangl
Members: Daniel T. Scannell, First Vice Chair; Lilyan H. Affinito; Laura D. Blackburne; Stanley Brezenoff; Warren S. Dolny; Thomas F. Egan; Barry Feinstein; Barbara J. Fife; Herbert J. Libert; Richard T. Nasti; Lucius J. Riccio; Joan Spence; Edward A. Vrooman; Robert F. Wagner, Jr.; Alfred E. Werner

President: Charles W. Hoppe
Jamaica Station, Mail Code 1137
Jamaica, New York 11435
Telephone: (718) 990-8252   Telefax: (718) 990-8212

Purchasing Agent: William Garrison, Director
Contracts, Procurement & Material Management
Jamaica Station, Mail Code 1437
Jamaica, New York 11435
Telephone: (718) 990-7760   Telefax: (718) 990-7839

Sum of Annual figures for 1990-1996   ** Ridership and financial figures in thousands.

Metro-North Commuter Railroad

In 1983 when Metro-North commuter Railroad was created from the remnants of Conrail's passenger division, it made a promise, to itself and to the public it serves, to provide reliable, comfortable and safe rail service. In its eight-year existence, Metro-North revived a moribund railroad and in a classic turnaround, created a safe, efficient, and reliable railroad.

Metro-North serves the nation's preeminent station, Grand Central Terminal. From the heart of midtown Manhattan, the railroad's three lines head north and fan out. The scenic Hudson line extends 74 miles to Poughkeepsie. The 77-mile Harlem line ends at Dover Plains, and the 72-mile New Haven line takes its name from its eastern terminus. Service is also provided on three branch lines in Connecticut to New Canaan, Danbury and Waterbury. Two other lines, both west of the Hudson River, the Port Jervis and the Pascacl Valley lines, are operated for Metro-North under contract by New Jersey Transit.

The railroad began a capital rebuilding program and since 1983 has spent $1.7 billion in infrastructure and rolling stock. A major component of this program was the electrification of nearly 30 miles of Upper Harlem Line between North While Plains and Brewster North.

As a result of this rebuilding program, as well as significantly expanded service and continuously increasing reliability, annual ridership has grown steadily from 47.7 million in 1982 to 56.5 million in 1990.

The railroad, along with its parent agency, the Metropolitan Transportation Authority, is now seeking New York State approval of a new capital program. Metro-North is seeking $935 million in capital funds for projects to be undertaken in the years 1992-1996. Among these projects are the modernization of utilities in Grand Central Terminal and rebuilding the badly deteriorated Park Avenue Viaduct, an elevated section of track in upper Manhattan that is the lifeline of the railroad.

	1985	1990	2000	*Projected 10-Year Total	Comments
Rail Ridership	50,270	57,641	67,421	627,004	Includes Port Jervis and Pascack Vally ridership.
Rail Agency Employees (Include Administrative Support)	6,100	6,099	6,189		
Track Miles	854	757	802°		Single track route miles. °Assumes approval of 1996 Capital Program.
Number of Rail Vehicles (All Types): In Operation	771	805	951°		
Refurbished	0	0	0	0	
Replaced	0	0	0	60	
**Annual Capital Budget (Rail Only)	$180,000	$171,000	$304,000	$2,476,000	
**Annual Operating Budget (Rail Only)	$409,135	$481,068	$860,700	$6,812,800	
**Total Rail Budget	$589,135	$652,068	$1,164,700	$9,288,800	
**Portion of Rail Budget Paid With Federal Funds if Available (Based on Current Law): Capital	$61,000	$38,000	$228,000	$1,857,000	
Operating	$11,500	$6,500	$14,000	$80,000	
Total	$72,500	$44,500	$242,000	$1,937,000	

Governing Board: **Metropolitan Transportation Authority Board of Directors**
347 Madison Avenue, 7th Floor
New York, New York 10017
Telephone: (212) 878-7446

Chair: Peter E. Stangl
Members: Daniel T. Scannell, First Vice Chair; Lilyan H. Affinito; Laura D. Blackburne; Stanley Brezenoff; Warren S. Dolny; Thomas F. Egan; Barry Feinstein; Barbara J. Fife; Herbert J. Libert; Richard T. Nasti; Lucius J. Riccio; Joan Spence; Edward A. Vrooman; Robert F. Wagner, Jr.; Alfred E. Werner

President: Donald Nelson
347 Madison Avenue, 12th Floor
New York, New York 10017
Telephone: (212) 340-2677

Purchasing Agent: Mary Ann Mills, Director Contract Administration and Procurement
347 Madison Avenue, 14th Floor
New York, New York 10017
Telephone: (212) 340-2495   Telefax: (212) 340-3250

Sum of Annual figures for 1991-2000.   ** Ridership and financial figures in thousands.

New York City Transit Authority

The New York City Transit Authority operates more trains to more stations and along more miles of track than any other urban rail system in the world. Providing 24-hour-a-day subway service throughout New York's five boroughs, the Authority's trains carry one billion passengers annually. Each weekday more than three and a half million subway trips are taken. About four out of every ten subway trips nationwide occur in New York City.

The subway system was originally managed by private companies. On October 27, 1904, the first subway ride for paying passengers took place in Manhattan. By 1940 the city had purchased two bankrupt companies to become the sole owner and operator of New York's subway and elevated lines. In 1953 the New York State Legislature created the Transit Authority as a separate public corporation to manage and operate these city-run subway routes.

During the fiscal crisis of the 1970s and early 1980s, the system was not maintained or routinely upgraded. As a result, the Authority faced a crisis of failing equipment as well as deteriorating track, stations and plant facilities.

With the help of federal, city and state capital program investments, the New York City Transit Authority has made a great deal of progress reinvigorating a bus and subway system on the verge of collapse. Between 1982 and 1991, the Transit Authority has over-hauled and replaced its subway fleet, the mainline track and many maintenance facilities.

However, much work remains to be done. More than half of the system's infrastructure has yet to achieve a state of good repair.

	1985	1990	2000	*Projected 10-Year Total	Comments
**Rail Ridership	1,010,211	1,027,936	1,113,000	10,657,000	Excludes effect of future fare increases
Rail Agency Employees (Include Administrative Support)	31,000	30,000	29,000		
Track Miles	684.2	697.7	698.3		Double track Excludes 106.5 miles in yards
Number of Rail Vehicles (All Types): In Operation	6,125	5,951	6,280		
Refurbished	531	479	0	806	
Replaced	376	0	170	1092	
**Annual Capital Budget (Rail Only)	$1,043,000	$1,184,000	$1,664,000	$15,008,000	
**Annual Operating Budget (Rail Only)	$1,532,800	$1,743,400	$2,300,000	$20,500,000	
**Total Rail Budget	$2,575,800	$2,927,400	$3,964,000	$35,508,000	
**Portion of Rail Budget Paid With Federal Funds if Available (Based on Current Law): Capital	$289,000	$404,000	$1,248,000	$11,256,000	33% UMTA assistance expected
Operating	$83,400	$72,400	$69,000	$615,000	
Total	$372,000	$476,000	$1,317,000	$11,871,000	

Governing Board: Metropolitan Transportation Authority Board of Directors
347 Madison Avenue, 7th Floor
New York, New York 10017
Telephone: (212) 878-7000   Telefax: (212) 878-7030

Chair: Peter E. Stangl
Members: Daniel T. Scannell, First Vice Chair; Lilyan H. Affinito; Laura D. Blackburne; Stanley Brezenoff; Warren S. Dolny; Thomas F. Egan; Barry Feinstein; Barbara J. Fife; Herbert J. Libert; Richard T. Nasti; Lucius J. Riccio; Joan Spence; Edward A. Vrooman; Robert F. Wagner, Jr.; Alfred E. Werner

President: Alan F. Kiepper
370 Jay Street
Brooklyn, New York 11201
Telephone: (718) 330-4321   Telefax: (718) 330-8998

Purchasing Agent: Dennis Erkus, Deputy Vice President, Purchasing
25 Chapel Street, Room 601
Brooklyn, New York 11201
Telephone: (718) 330-4800   Telefax: (718) 935-0804

Sum of Annual figures for 1991-2000.   ** Ridership and financial figures in thousands.

Niagara Frontier Transportation Authority

Public rail transit in Buffalo, New York, goes back nearly 160 years when, in 1832, the first horse-drawn streetcars went into operation. They traveled on wooden rails topped with iron straps. By the 1870s, the city's horsecar routes were serving more than five million passengers a year. By 1922 the street rail transit system had extended to 202 miles.

Following World War II, and coinciding with the nation's love affair with the private automobile, ridership declined. A massive population shift from the city to the suburbs compounded transit's problems. In July 1950 Buffalo's system became all bus.

In 1967, recognizing the severe financial difficulties being encountered by privately owned transit companies, the State of New York created the Niagara Frontier Transportation Authority (NFTA), a public benefit corporation owned by the citizens. Its mission was to formulate and implement a unified area mass transportation policy.

Contemporary transit planners first began thinking of modern rail transit in the mid-1960s as an alternative to land-devouring highways. Construction of a rail rapid transit line in Buffalo began in 1979, creating hundreds of badly needed jobs, with much of the $535 million cost being spent in the Western New York area.

The 6.4-mile rail line opened in May 1985. It brought about a resurgence of downtown activity and was a catalyst for major development. Today planners are developing long-range projects, capitalizing on the area's greatest asset, its undeveloped waterfront. Fully integrated rail and bus transportation, prepared to meet present and future needs, will keep the area moving, and future extensions to its rail spine are key!

Niagara Frontier Transportation Authority (NFTA)

	1985[0]	1990	2000	*Projected 10-Year Total	Comments
Rail Ridership	—	8,480	15,400[1]	120,000[1]	[0]System began May 1985
Rail Agency Employees (Include Administrative Support)	—	170	226		[1]Assumes annual growth of 100,000 on existing line
Track Miles	—	13	26		6-mile double track extension
Number of Rail Vehicles (All Types): In Operation	—	27	40		Additional cars needed for extension
Refurbished	—	0	0	0	
Replaced	—	0	0	0	
Annual Capital Budget (Rail Only)	—	$2,686	$4,000	$400,000	Construction of 6-mile extension anticipated
Annual Operating Budget (Rail Only)	—	$11,806	$22,000	$160,000	
Total Rail Budget	—	$14,492	$26,000	$560,000	
Portion of Rail Budget Paid With Federal Funds if Available (Based on Current Law): Capital	—	$282	$2,500	$300,000	
Operating	—	$1,525	$1,525	$15,250	
Total	—	$1,807	$4,025	$315,250	

Governing Board: **Niagara Frontier Transportation Authority Board of Commissioners**
181 Ellicott Street
Buffalo, New York 14203

Chair: Robert D.Gioia
Members: James H. Wolford, Vice Chair; George L. Wessel, Treasurer;
Theodore D. Williamson, Sr., Secretary; Ronald J. Anthony; William G. Gisel;
Ernestine R. Green; David N. Greenfield; Marilyn Royer; James M. Wadsworth

Executive Director: Richard T. Swist
181 Ellicott Street
Buffalo, New York 14203
Telephone: (716) 855-7230

Purchasing Agent: John Gross, Manager Materiels & Procurement
181 Ellicott Street
Buffalo, New York 14203
Telephone: (716) 855-7353

---

*Sum of Annual figures for 1991-2000.   ** Ridership and financial figures in thousands.

Port Authority Trans-Hudson System (PATH)

The Port Authority Trans-Hudson System (PATH) is the primary rail transit link between Manhattan and neighboring New Jersey urban communities and suburban commuter railroads. Over 200,000 customers travel on PATH each week day on more than 1,100 train movements. The system has four lines and 13 station along 42.8 miles of track, over half of it underground. Opened in 1908 as the Hudson and Manhattan Railroad, PATH has been the rail subsidiary of the Port Authority of New York and New Jersey since 1962.

PATH is in the final stages of a $1 billion Capital Improvement Program which has included the complete renewal of the PATH fleet: its 247 existing cars were rebuilt; 95 new cars were added; and a $205 million state-of-the-art car maintenance facility began operations in October 1990. Major improvements also have been completed at six PATH stations. Station upgrades include grand entrance pavilions, new escalators, handsome works of art and the first video news and passenger information system in the New Jersey-New York region. Work is now underway at seven stations to make them more accessible to the elderly and mobility impaired.

Construction of three new electrical substations and installation of a new power supervisory control system are in progress. Also underway is a new tunnel emergency ventilation system to improve the flow of smoke and fresh air in the event of an emergency.

PATH is currently phasing in <u>QuickCard</u>, a magnetically coded fare card. A joint ticketing arrangement with New Jersey Transit represents a new era for mass transportation in the region as a first step in establishing a seamless mass transit network on both sides of the Hudson River. PATH is a prime mover in developing a transportation network in the New Jersey-New York metropolitan area that is safe, fast, efficient, reliable and integrated with other systems in order to provide its customers with better service and more ease and convenience than ever before.

Port Authority Trans-Hudson System (PATH)

	1985	1990	2000	*Projected 10-Year Total	Comments
**Rail Ridership	54,000	56,000	61,000	581,000	
Rail Agency Employees (Include Administrative Support)	1,129	1,184	1,200		
Track Miles	35.3	42.8	47.8		Single track
Number of Rail Vehicles (All Types): In Operation	288	342	342		
Refurbished	0°	0	0	0	°From 1985-1989, 95 new cars were added to the fleet, and 247 cars were completely rehabilitated.
Replaced	0°	0	0	0	
**Annual Capital Budget (Rail Only)	$55,000	$168,000	$70,000	$720,000	
**Annual Operating Budget (Rail Only)	$102,000	$133,000	$315,000	$2,500,000	
**Total Rail Budget	$157,000	$301,000	$385,000	$3,220,000	
**Portion of Rail Budget Paid With Federal Funds if Available (Based on Current Law): Capital	$0	$0	$0	$0	
Operating	$0	$0	$0	$0	PATH operations are supported by revenues of the Port Authority of NY & NJ
Total	$0	$0	$0	$0	

Governing Board: Port Authority Trans-Hudson Corporation Board of Directors
1 World Trade Center - 62W
New York, New York 10048
Telephone: (212) 435-7664   Telefax: (212) 466-6347

President: Stanley Brezenoff
Chair: Richard C. Leone
Members: Hazel Frank Gluck, James G. Hellmuth, Henry F. Henderson, Jr., William K. Hutchison, Philip D. Kaltenbacher, John G. McGoldrick, Basil A. Paterson, Howard Schulman, Robert Van Buren

Vice President & General Manager: Richard R. Kelly
1 World Trade Center - 62W
New York, New York 10048
Telephone: (212) 435-7664   Telefax: (212) 466-6347

Purchasing Agent: Alfred T. Robertson, Manager
Purchasing & Supply Services
1 World Trade Center - 82S
New York, New York 10048
Telephone: (212) 435-3900   Telefax: (212) 466-1090

* Sum of Annual figures for 1991-2000.   ** Ridership and financial figures in thousands.

Greater Cleveland Regional Transit Authority

Public transportation in greater Cleveland has a long and proud history. Early efforts included an 1818 stagecoach that ran between Cleveland and Painesville. Omnibus service — a carriage for large groups of riders — started in 1841, and Public Square saw horsecar service in 1834. Later, as electric trolleys gained popularity, Cleveland's transit system included 425 miles of streetcar lines. Smaller lines were consolidated in 1903 as the Cleveland Electric Railway Company.

Cleveland's rapid transit system started in 1913 when real estate tycoons, brothers O. P. and M. J. Van Sweringen, realized the need to provide their budding community with high-class rail transit service. Construction of the first tracks, which are now the Green and Blue Lines, began in 1913 and was completed in 1920.

Work on the Red Line began at Windermere in 1952 and continued until 1968, when the tracks reached Hopkins International Airport. That made Cleveland the first city in the Western Hemisphere to offer rapid transit service to its major airport.

Today the RTA is a multimodal system consisting of light rail, heavy rail, buses and paratransit. The light rail system travels between Tower City in downtown Cleveland and Shaker Square where the two lines branch off in separate directions. There are 29 stations on the Blue and Green Lines. The light rail system was rebuilt in 1981 at a cost of $100 million. The heavy rail system is called the Red Line and runs from Windermere Rapid Station in East Cleveland westward to Tower City and out to the terminal at Cleveland Hopkins International Airport. There are 18 stations on the Red Line. Renovations to all the stations are planned, with $70 million to be invested in this system over the next five years. Combined, the rail system employs 106 train operators and 35 booth attendants. The RTA has 48 light rail and 60 heavy rail cars to cover a weekday peak requirement of 70 cars.

GREATER CLEVELAND REGIONAL TRANSIT AUTHORITY (RTA)

	1985	1990	2000	*Projected 10-Year Total	Comments
**Rail Ridership	10,123	8,891	11,125	104,677	
Rail Agency Employees (Include Administrative Support)	409	472	472		
Track Miles	65.44	65.44	65.44		Double track
Number of Rail Vehicles (All Types): In Operation	108	108	108		
Refurbished	0	0	0	0	
Replaced	0	0	0	0	
**Annual Capital Budget (Rail Only)	$4,375	$38,704	$47,013	$557,161	
**Annual Operating Budget (Rail Only)	$18,176	$23,210	$33,655	$369,623	
**Total Rail Budget	$22,551	$61,914	$80,668	$926,784	
**Portion of Rail Budget Paid With Federal Funds if Available (Based on Current Law): Capital	$1,929	$30,963	$37,610	$445,729	
Operating	$1,727	$1,416	$2,053	$22,547	
Total	$3,656	$32,379	$39,663	$468,276	

Governing Board: Greater Cleveland Regional Transit Authority Board of Trustees
615 Superior Northwest
Cleveland, Ohio 44113
Telephone: (216) 566-5100   Telefax: (216) 241-8307

President: Hon. Earl Martin
Members: Deborah E. Perkins, Vice President; Jesse O. Anderson; Hon. Thomas J. Coyne;
Rebecca Devenanzio; Francisco Molina; Janie L. Rollins; Mark Ruzic; Marjorie B. Wright

General Manager/ Secretary-Treasurer: Ronald J. Tober
615 Superior Northwest
Cleveland, Ohio 44113
Telephone: (216) 566-5100   Telefax: (216) 241-8307

Purchasing Agent: James Zingale, Director of Procurement
615 Superior Northwest
Cleveland, Ohio 44113
Telephone: (216) 566-5100   Telefax: (216) 566-0856

Sum of Annual figures for 1991-2000.   ** Ridership and financial figures in thousands.   97

Tri-County Metropolitan Transportation District of Oregon (Tri-Met)

Portland's first interurban rail line opened in 1893, connecting Portland and Oregon City. By 1915 it had been joined by more than 200 miles of trolley service, and the Portland area had the third most extensive electric railway system in America. The Oregon City line would ply its daily course until 1958, when the last trolleys were replaced by diesel buses.

By 1978 the city again turned to rail to preserve a treasure in danger of being lost: Portland's cherished quality of life. Citizens organized to oppose a proposed freeway threatening to destroy their neighborhood — in exchange for nothing more than increased traffic congestion and air pollution. They convinced elected officials to withdraw the freeway from the federal interstate system, but keep the construction funds committed to transportation improvements in the metro area. Those funds financed Portland's first modern rail line and more than 110 miles of highway improvements in the Portland area.

In 1978 local governments approved construction of a 15-mile light rail line between Portland and Gresham, a growing suburb to the east.

Christened "MAX" at its opening in September 1986, Tri-Met's Metropolitan Area Express is widely recognized to be one of the most successful new rail projects in the country. MAX has become a popular part of Portland's urban landscape, helping to inspire over $1 billion in development along its tracks and carrying an average of 22,000 weekday boardings — and close to 50,000 on its busiest days.

Today, MAX has an approval rating of 96%. Last November, voters approved a bond measure to help finance MAX expansion by an overwhelming margin of three-to-one.

The Regional Transportation Plan calls for a system of rail lines serving six congested corridors. The next project is an 18-mile extension to Hillsboro, serving Washington County, the fastest growing part of the state which contains Oregon's "Silicon Forest" of burgeoning high-tech companies.

TRI-COUNTY METROPOLITAN TRANSPORTATION DISTRICT (TRI-MET)

	1985	1990	2000	*Projected 10-Year Total	Comments
**Rail Ridership	—	6,720	17,495	98,065	Reflects Westside opening in 1997
Rail Agency Employees (Include Administrative Support)	—	113	209		
Track Miles	—	15.1	33.1		Double track
Number of Rail Vehicles (All Types): In Operation	—	26	70		
Refurbished	—	0	0	0	
Replaced	—	0	0	0	
**Annual Capital Budget (Rail Only)	$81,862	$79,068	$127,898	$1,043,733	
**Annual Operating Budget (Rail Only)	—	$6,869	$18,099	$122,763	
**Total Rail Budget	$81,862	$13,292	$37,299	$1,166,496	
**Portion of Rail Budget Paid With Federal Funds if Available (Based on Current Law): Capital	—	$47,441	$76,382	$832,588	
Operating	—	$261	$543	$3,131	
Total	—	$47,702	$76,925	$835,719	

Governing Board: Tri-County Metropolitan Transit District Board of Directors
4012 S. E. 17th Avenue
Portland, Oregon 97202
Telephone: (503) 238-4831   Telefax: (503) 239-6451

President: Loren Wyss
Members: William Robertson, Vice President; Philip Bogue, Treasurer; Robert Bocci; Nita Brueggeman; Gary Conkling; Ron Tonkin

General Manager: Thomas J. Walsh
4012 S. E. 17th Avenue
Portland, Oregon 97202
Telephone: (503) 238-4951   Telefax: (503) 239-6451

Purchasing Agent: Ron Imondi, Purchasing Manager
4012 S. E. 17th Avenue
Portland, Oregon 97202
Telephone: (503) 238-4993   Telefax: (503) 239-6467

Sum of Annual figures for 1991-2000.   ** Ridership and financial figures in thousands.

Cambria County Transit Authority

Millions of tourists from around the world have visited the famous Johnstown Inclined Plane, one of the steepest vehicular inclined planes in the world.

The Inclined Plane opened June 1, 1891. Built in the aftermath of the Great Johnstown Flood of 1889, it has delighted countless visitors ever since. The two 15-foot wide, 34-foot long incline cars stand straight out in the air above the steep 71.9% grade as they go up and down the mountain. The cars are pulled by two-inch cables, designed after the system used in the 1800s to move canal boats over the craggy Allegheny Mountains. The Inclined Plane was originally powered by a large steam engine which was replaced in the 1920s by a 400 horsepower electric motor.

The original Inclined Plane was constructed by the Cambria Iron Company, manufacturers of the first iron railroad rails in the United States. Cambria Iron and its successor, the Bethlehem Steel Corporation, operated the hillside railway until 1923, when it was sold to Westmont Borough for $1.00. In 1982 the badly deteriorated Incline was sold to the Cambria County Transit Authority, which totally rebuilt the system at a cost of $3.5 million. Today, the Inclined Plane is a vital link in Johnstown's mass transit system.

In 1990 a major addition to the hillside was completed with the addition of the Inclined Plane Visitors' Center. The glass-walled top floor contains special displays to inform visitors about the region's many tourist attractions. The bottom floor features the unique Incline Station Restaurant & Pub, with each table affording a panoramic view of the valley below. The hillside also flies a 30' x 60' American Flag, one of the largest free-flying flags in the U.S. A new observation deck, towering over the Inclined Plane hillside, offers a fantastic view of the valley below.

	1985	1990	2000	*Projected 10-Year Total	Comments
**Rail Ridership	71	205	246	2,255°	°APTA estimate
Rail Agency Employees (Include Administrative Support)	9	9	9		
Track Miles	.17	.17	.17		Double track
Number of Rail Vehicles (All Types): In Operation	2	2	2		
Refurbished	0	0	0	0	
Replaced	0	0	0	0	
**Annual Capital Budget (Rail Only)	$3,200	$2,213	$715	$1,200°	
**Annual Operating Budget (Rail Only)	$88	$216	$281	$2,500°	
**Total Rail Budget	$3,288	$2429	$996	$3,700°	
**Portion of Rail Budget Paid With Federal Funds if Available (Based on Current Law): Capital	$2,400	$308	$536	$900	
Operating	$0	$0	$140	$600	
Total	$2,400	$308	$676	$1,500	

Governing Board: **Cambria County Transit Authority Board of Directors**
726 Central Avenue
Johnstown, Pennsylvania 15902-2996
Telephone: (814) 535-5526

Chair: Frank J. Castelli
Members: Ernest E. Wadsworth, Vice Chair; Regina Winslow, Secretary; Jack W. Shearer, Assistant Secretary; Edward P. Trofino, Treasurer; Joseph J. McAneny, Assistant Treasurer; Margaret L. Armbruster; Edward J. Cernic, Sr.; Senator William J. Stewart

General Manager: Harold C. Jenkins
726 Central Avenue
Johnstown, Pennsylvania 15902-2996
Telephone: (814) 535-5526

Purchasing Agent: David Edwards
726 Central Avenue
Johnstown, Pennsylvania 15902-2996
Telephone: (814) 535-5526

Sum of Annual figures for 1991-2000.   ** Ridership and financial figures in thousands.

Port Authority of Allegheny County (PAT)

PAT's light rail transit system, "The T," continues a century-long tradition of providing rail service to citizens in the southern portion of Allegheny County.

While the system represents only a small fraction of the total rail system that once operated in the County, it transports in excess of ten percent of PAT's daily riders on its three routes and 71 rail cars. Unexpectedly high peak-hour ridership resulted in implementation of two-car trains as well as an effort to secure additional parking spaces for would-be patrons.

The system is made up of a diverse number of elements: single and double trackage, trackage on right-of-way, on city streets, in two tunnels and a downtown subway. Portions of the system that were not reconstructed during the Stage I project appear as they did in the 1940s and provide a striking contrast to the new cars and technology employed in the post-1985 portion of the 22.5-mile system. While this combination of new and old technologies makes the PAT system unique, it shares with one system (New Orleans) and one trolley museum (Arden, in Washington, Pennsylvania) the distinction of operating on a track gauge of 5 feet, 2 1/2 inches.

The exact track the system will take in the future remains uncertain; studies will help shape the future for modernization of the older portions of the system as well as possible extensions from Downtown to near North Side and from Downtown to the east, serving the Oakland/Squirrel Hill areas.

	1985	1990	2000	*Projected 10-Year Total	Comments
**Rail Ridership	2,577	9,840	13,980	134,031	
Rail Agency Employees (Include Administrative Support)	403	393	400		
Track Miles	28	22	28		Double track
Number of Rail Vehicles (All Types): In Operation	49	71	65		
Refurbished	0	16	0	0	
Replaced	0	0	0	10	
**Annual Capital Budget (Rail Only)		$2,859°	$4,657°	$37,754°	
**Annual Operating Budget (Rail Only)	$19,893	$23,904	$35,900	$298,449	°Figures exclude spending for rail rehabilitation projects.
**Total Rail Budget	$19,893	$26,763	$40,557	$336,203	
**Portion of Rail Budget Paid With Federal Funds if Available (Based on Current Law): Capital		$2,287°	$3,725°	$33,923°	
Operating	$1,144	$1,352	$2,000	$15,006	
Total	$1,144	$3,639	$5,725	$48,929	

Governing Board: **Port Authority of Allegheny County Board of Directors**
2235 Beaver Avenue
Pittsburgh, Pennsylvania 15233
Telephone: (412) 237-7000   Telefax: (412) 237-7101

Chair: John P. Robin
Board of Directors: Robert P. Argentine, Neal H. Holmes, Laura Horgan,
Joseph A. Katarincic, James N. Kratsa, Garland H. McAdoo, Jr., Robert P. Pease,
Marilyn Skolnick

General Manager: William W. Millar
2235 Beaver Avenue
Pittsburgh, Pennsylvania 15233
Telephone: (412) 237-7000   Telefax: (412) 237-7101

Purchasing Agent: Terry Johnson, Manager of Procurement
2235 Beaver Avenue
Pittsburgh, Pennsylvania 15233
Telephone: (412) 237-7000   Telefax: (412) 237-7101

Sum of Annual figures for 1991-2000.   ** Ridership and financial figures in thousands.

Southeastern Pennsylvania Transportation Authority (SEPTA)

SEPTA began operating Philadelphia's transit services in 1969, including a light rail system dating from 1858, and a subway-elevated system started in 1907. In 1970 the Authority moved into suburban operations which include two light rail routes and the interurban Norristown High Speed Line. It was not until 1983 that SEPTA took over operation of southeastern Pennsylvania's extensive, turn-of-the-century regional rail system which now has seven routes.

Notable rail improvements in recent years include partial replacement of the light rail subway-elevated and regional rail fleets; the opening of a new Center City station as part of a tunnel now connecting two former stub-end, six-lane systems; inauguration of regional rail service between Center City and Philadelphia International Airport; and the extension of two regional rail routes over existing rights-of-way.

But there has been a gradual decline in SEPTA rail services during the last decade, caused by a lack of capital funds to replace the deteriorating old systems. A number of streetcar routes in Philadelphia have been converted (some temporarily and some permanently) to bus routes because they can no longer be operated safely. Several sections of the regional rail system have also been cut off for the same reason.

There are two basic causes for continuing infrastructure deterioration and system shrinkage: a 75% decline in federal support since 1978, and a lack of predictable, dedicated funding in Pennsylvania. The Commonwealth is the only transit-dependent state in the Union that does not provide such funding.

SEPTA's 1991-2000 Capital Program is a $4.5 billion "Action Plan for the 90s" which, if funded, will renew the transit and regional rail systems and "set the stage for bold initiatives for expanded service in the 21st Century."

SOUTHEASTERN PENNSYLVANIA TRANSPORTATION AUTHORITY (SEPTA)

	1985°	1990	2000	*Projected 10-Year Total	Comments
**Rail Ridership	115,685	110,411	105,000	1,070,000[1]	° Fiscal year 1986 [1] APTA estimate
Rail Agency Employees (Include Administrative Support)	1,470 SC 1,952 RR 1,723 CR	1,185 SC 1,908 RR 1,701 CR	5,200		SC = Streetcar RR = Rapid rail CR = Commuter rail
Track Miles	173 SC 87 RR 620 CR	172 SC 87 RR 694 CR	173 SC 91 RR 789 CR		Single track route miles. Portions of track are leased from Amtrak and Conrail.
Number of Rail Vehicles (All Types): In Operation	980	994	1022		
Refurbished	0	62	50	396	
Replaced	0	0	0	410	
**Annual Capital Budget (Rail Only)	$255,000	$294,000	$362,300	$3,623,000	Rail portion of $4.5 billion Action Plan
**Annual Operating Budget (Rail Only)	$159,759	$219,726	$420,942	$3,307,674	
**Total Rail Budget	$414,759	$513,726	$783,242	$6,930,674	
**Portion of Rail Budget Paid With Federal Funds if Available (Based on Current Law): Capital	$191,250	$205,800	$271,000	$2,710,000	Assumes 75% capital match per federal law.
Operating	$11,000	$9,600	$9,600	$96,000	
Total	$202,250	$215,400	$280,600	$3,806,000	

<u>Governing Board:</u> **Southeastern Pennsylvania Transportation Authority Board of Directors**
714 Market Street
Philadelphia, Pennsylvania 19107
Telephone: (215) 580-4000   Telefax: (215) 580-7328

Chair: J. Clayton Undercofler
Members: Judith E. Harris, Vice Chair; Floriana Bloss; Mary Harris;
Thomas Hayward; Frank Jenkins; Edmund Jones; Richard Kurtz; Andrew Warren;
Franklin Wood

<u>Chief Operations Officer/</u>
<u>General Manager:</u> Louis J. Gambaccini
714 Market Street
Philadelphia, Pennsylvania 19107
Telephone: (215) 580-4000   Telefax: (215) 580-7328

<u>Purchasing Agent:</u> John T. Prader, Assistant General Manager, Material and Contracts
200 W. Wyoming Avenue
Philadelphia, Pennsylvania 19140
Telephone: (215) 580-4300   Telefax: (215) 580-4333

Sum of Annual figures for 1991-2000.   ** Ridership and financial figures in thousands.

Chattanooga Area Regional Transportation Authority (CARTA)

In addition to its regular bus transit service, CARTA owns and operates the Lookout Mountain Incline Railway. The Incline serves as a major tourist attraction as well as a means of public transportation for area residents. Carrying over 300,000 persons annually, the Incline generates net revenue which defers a portion of CARTA's operating expenses.

The Incline opened for business on November 16, 1895. It was the third railway developed to link the newly thriving tourist developments on the top of Lookout Mountain with the Chattanooga valley below. The track is almost one mile long and goes straight up the side of Lookout Mountain, reaching a 72.7% grade at its steepest point near the top, giving the Incline the distinction of being the world's steepest passenger railway. Because of the important role the Incline played in the historical development of the area, it was named a National Historic Site in 1974.

The Incline cars currently in operation were installed in 1987. The cars were especially designed and built at an 18-degree angle. Each car is steel, carries 44 passengers, is 42 feet long and weighs 12 tons. Two 1 1/4-inch wire cables carry the cars up and down the mountain. The cables are fastened underneath one car, wound around huge drums in the machine room at the top of the mountain, and connected underneath the other car so that the two cars operate like weights on a pulley — when one car goes up, the other goes down. The entire cable system is changed every three years.

CHATTANOOGA AREA REGIONAL TRANSPORTATION AUTHORITY (CARTA)

	1985	1990	2000	*Projected 10-Year Total	Comments
. **Rail Ridership	289	358	457	4,075	
2. Rail Agency Employees (Include Administrative Support)	8	8	8		
3. Track Miles	1	1	1		Double track
. Number of Rail Vehicles (All Types): In Operation	2	2	2		
Refurbished	0	0	0	2	
Replaced	0	0	0	0	Both cars were replaced in 1987
5. **Annual Capital Budget (Rail Only)	$466	$84	$150	$1,875	
6. **Annual Operating Budget (Rail Only)	$530	$676	$1,022	$8,681	
7. **Total Rail Budget	$996	$760	$1,172	$10,556	
8. **Portion of Rail Budget Paid With Federal Funds if Available (Based on Current Law): Capital	$373	$67	$120	$1,500	
Operating	$143	$122	$204	$1,736	
Total	$516	$189	$324	$3,236	

Governing Board: Chattanooga Area Regional Transportation Authority Board of Directors
1617 Wilcox Boulevard
Chattanooga, Tennessee 37406
Telephone: (615) 629-1411   Telefax: (615) 698-2749

Chair: Frederick L. Hitchcock
Members: Robert C. Diehl, Don T. Hart, E. Stephen Jett, Isabel Langley, Randolph C. Martin, Sr., Carrington Montague, Harry E. Tate, Donald C. Thompson, Shelburne Warren

Executive Director: Thomas W. Dugan
1617 Wilcox Boulevard
Chattanooga, Tennessee 37406
Telephone: (615) 629-1411   Telefax: (615) 698-2749

Purchasing Agent: Roger Tudor, Director of Purchasing
1617 Wilcox Boulevard
Chattanooga, Tennessee 37406
Telephone: (615) 629-1411   Telefax: (615) 698-2749

Sum of Annual figures for 1991-2000.   ** Ridership and financial figures in thousands.

Dallas Area Rapid Transit (DART)

Public Transportation in the city of Dallas dates back to 1871, when two street cars pulled by mules provided service to the county courthouse. Steam-powered cars provided service until 1891, when electrically powered trolley cars began service in the inner city. In 1956 the Dallas streetcar made its final run. It was replaced by diesel buses operated by several companies before being purchased by the City of Dallas in 1965. Seventeen years later, 14 cities in the Dallas area voted in favor of Dallas Area Rapid Transit. A voter-approved one-cent sales tax went into effect January 1, 1984. Two other cities joined DART in 1985, bringing total membership to 16 cities. A 25-member board of directors was appointed by area city councils.

DART's service area encompasses 700 square miles. The agency operates local and express bus service, HandRides van service for the mobility-impaired, DARTAbout demand-responsive van service, and provides $13 million each year in capital assistance for general mobility projects and technical assistance through the Local Assistance Program.

Following three years of development and revision, DART held an election for the use of long-term debt to finance construction of a 93-mile light rail system through the year 2010. Although the vote failed, DART began working with the community to develop a balanced transit plan requiring no long-term debt. In June 1989 a new plan was adopted, including 67 miles of light rail (20 miles to be open by 1997), 18 miles of commuter rail and 37 miles of High Occupancy Vehicle (HOV) lanes for construction by the year 2010. Under the financial plan established, DART would pay 80% of the capital costs with a 20% federal funding requirement to build the system. On October 12, 1990, DART's first rail-related construction began with relocation of a downtown Dallas street to make way for light rail installation.

In the Dallas area, the future is riding on DART.

	1985	1990	2000	*Projected 10-Year Total	Comments
**Rail Ridership	—	—	11,099	38,000	Rail construction began October 1990
Rail Agency Employees (Include Administrative Support)	—	—	200		
Track Miles	—	—	38^0		^{0}Double track 20 miles LRT 18 miles Com. Rail
Number of Rail Vehicles (All Types): In Operation	—	—	100^1		^{1}90 LRT 10 Com. Rail
Refurbished	—	—	0	0	
Replaced	—	—	0	0	
**Annual Capital Budget (Rail Only)	—	—	$199,700	$1,759,600	
**Annual Operating Budget (Rail Only)	—	—	$62,700	$1,500,000	
**Total Rail Budget	—	—	$262,400	$3,259,600	
**Portion of Rail Budget Paid With Federal Funds if Available (Based on Current Law): Capital	—	—	$36,600	$330,000	
Operating	—	—	$0	$0	DART receives no operating assistance for rail operations.
Total	—	—	$36,600	$330,000	

Governing Board:

Dallas Area Rapid Transit Board of Directors
c/o Executive Assistant to the Board of Directors, Attn. Nancy McKethan
601 Pacific Avenue, 7th Floor
Dallas, Texas 75202
Telephone: (214) 658-6237

Chair: Marvin M. Lane, Jr.
Members: Raymond Noah, Vice Chair; Don Raines, Secretary; J.B. Jackson, Assistant Secreatry; Michael Campbell; Jerry Fitzgerald; Liz Flores-Velasquez; Jerome Garza; Kenn George; Henry Graeser; Sandy Greyson; Kathy Ingle; Jim Jenne, June E. Lykes; Robert McElearney; Anne McKinney; Dan Monaghan; Cipriano Munoz; Robert Price; DeMetris Sampson; Norma Stanton; Charles Terrell, Jr.; Bruce C. Toal; Jim Williams

Executive Director:

Charles S. Anderson
601 Pacific Avenue
Dallas, Texas 75202
Telephone: (214) 658-6201   Telefax: (214) 658-6211

Purchasing Agent:

Christopher Poinsatte, Assistant Executive Director, Procurement
601 Pacific Avenue
Dallas, Texas 75202
Telephone: (214) 658-6196   Telefax: (214) 658-6558

Sum of Annual figures for 1991-2000.   ** Ridership and financial figures in thousands.

Metropolitan Transit Authority of Harris County

The Metropolitan Transit Authority of Harris County (METRO) was created in 1977 by the Texas State Legislature. In 1978 the voters of Harris County approved a one-cent sales tax to support construction of a mass transit system, and the agency began operations in 1979. METRO has developed one of the most highly acclaimed bus systems in North America and is the national leader in developing high occupancy vehicle lanes (HOVs).

In January 1988 voters in METRO's service area approved a thirteen-year program, "The Phase 2 Mobility Plan," to provide a balanced solution to Houston's transportation problems. Under this program METRO will expand its top-quality bus system; dedicate 25% of its sales tax revenue to the construction of streets and roadways; complete the 95.5-mile HOV system; and build the first 24 miles of a rail system.

In March 1991 the METRO Board of Directors selected a monorail technology for the first of three rail lines to be built by the Authority as part of the Phase 2 Mobility Plan. With construction beginning in the summer of 1993, the first 14-mile segment is planned to be completed by 1998. By the year 2000 METRO is scheduled to have all 24 miles of rail in operation.

With this Phase 2 program in progress, METRO is entering a new era with excitement and optimism. There are great days ahead for Houston and METRO. We're on the move!

	1985	1990	2000	*Projected 10-Year Total	Comments
Rail Ridership	—	—	15,400	40,600	1998 is first year of service
Rail Agency Employees (Include Administrative Support)	—	—			
Track Miles	—	—	23.5		Double Track
Number of Rail Vehicles (All Types): In Operation	—	—			
Refurbished	—	—	0	0	
Replaced	—	—	0	0	
**Annual Capital Budget (Rail Only)	—	—	$58,040	$1,089,793	All financial figures in constant 1988 dollars
**Annual Operating Budget (Rail Only)	—	—	$14,711	$38,854	
**Total Rail Budget	—	—	$72,751	$1,128,647	
**Portion of Rail Budget Paid With Federal Funds if Available (Based on Current Law): Capital	—	—	$29,020	$544,897	
Operating	—	—	$0	$0	
Total	—	—	$29,020	$544,897	

Governing Board: Metropolitan Transit Authority of Harris County Board of Directors
1201 Louisiana , 23rd floor
Houston, Texas 77002
Telephone: (713) 739-4840

Chair: Anthony W. Hall, Jr.
Members: Alfonso Matta, Vice Chair; P. J. Lionetti, Secretary; William F. Burge III;
Don R. Caggins; Newton J. Calvin, Jr.; John T. Cater; Charles W. Duncan, Jr.

General Manager: Robert G. MacLennan
P. O. Box 61429
Houston, Texas 77208-1429
Telephone: (713) 739-4830   Telefax: (713) 739-4697

Virginia Railway Express

The Virginia Railway Express (VRE) is a "new start" commuter rail venture connecting the jurisdictions of Northern Virginia to the District of Columbia. The VRE is jointly sponsored by two regional transportation commissions, the Northern Virginia Transportation Commission (NVTC) and the Potomac and Rappahannock Transportation Commission (PRTC), and is overseen by the VRE Operations Board consisting of members from the Commissions and Virginia Department of Transportation.

The VRE will consist of approximately 100 route miles. Existing Norfolk Southern freight trackage will be used to convey VRE trains between Manassas, Virginia and the District. The northern terminus of the service will be Union Station in Washington. Amtrak will operate the service and maintain equipment on behalf of the VRE.

As jurisdictions join the sponsoring Commissions in the future, additional stations will join the seventeen envisioned for the start of service in the Spring of 1992. Stations, yards, rolling stock, ticket vending machines and other capital items amounting to approximately $127 million are funded through a combination of bond proceeds, contributions from the jurisdictions and funding from the State.

	1985	1992°	2000	*Projected 8-Year Total[1]	Comments
**Rail Ridership	—	2,250	5,750	35,982	°1992 is 1st year of operation.
Rail Agency Employees (Include Administrative Support)	—	65[2]	105[2]		[1]All projected totals are for 8 years. [2]Includes contract personnel.
Track Miles	—	100	100		Double and service track.
Number of Rail Vehicles (All Types): In Operation	—	73	126		
Refurbished	—	0	0	38	
Replaced	—	0	0	25	
**Annual Capital Budget (Rail Only)	—	$6,700	$10,000	$91,950	
**Annual Operating Budget (Rail Only)	—	$11,000	$22,000	$148,500	
**Total Rail Budget	—	$17,700	$32,000	$240,450	
**Portion of Rail Budget Paid With Federal Funds if Available (Based on Current Law): Capital	—	$0	$7,500	$68,963	
Operating	—	$0	$4,000	$32,000	
Total	—	$0	$11,500	$100,963	

Governing Board: The Virginia Railway Express has two sponsoring commissions and one supervisory board.

Northern Virginia Transportation Commission
4350 N. Fairfax Drive
Arlington, Virginia 22203
Chair: Ellen Bozman

Potomac and Rappanhannock Transportation Commission
12906 Occoquan Road
Woodbridge, Virginia 22192
Chair: Robert Cole

Virginia Railway Express Operations Board
4350 N. Fairfax Drive
Arlington, Virginia 22203
Telephone: (703) 524-3322   Telefax: (703) 524-1756
Chair: Sharon Bulova

Rail Manager: Thomas R. Waldron
4350 N. Fairfax Drive
Arlington, Virginia 22203
Telephone: (703) 524-3322   Telefax: (703) 524-1756

* Sum of Annual figures for 1992-2000.   ** Ridership and financial figures in thousands.

Municipality of Metropolitan Seattle (Metro Transit)

Streetcars, once an integral part of Seattle's transportation system, were replaced in the 1940s with the advent of rubber-tired buses. Due to the efforts of Metro and City Councilmember George Benson, a longtime transit supporter and streetcar fan, a streetcar system along Seattle's waterfront was constructed in 1982.

The Municipality of Metropolitan Seattle was created in 1958 to address the issue of countywide sewage treatment. In 1973 voters authorized Metro to assume responsibility for providing countywide transportation.

The streetcar system was built by the City of Seattle and operated by the Municipality of Metropolitan Seattle (Metro Transit) until 1986 when ownership of the streetcar line was transferred to Metro. At that time planning for an extension to the 1.6-mile line was initiated.

A 1/2-mile extension to the streetcar system was planned to connect the waterfront with two other activity centers in the downtown area, Pioneer Square and the International District, and to make a connection to the downtown bus tunnel under Third Avenue. The extension cost $6.5 million and was funded entirely with Metro funds. The extension opened in June 1991.

In addition to the streetcar system, Metro is currently investigating the feasibility of a high capacity transit system for north, south and east corridors in the region as part of the Metro 2000 Plan. The system could include a combination of busway and light rail technology. A decision on the technology and the phasing of corridor development is anticipated by 1992. The Metro 2000 Capital Plan will be submitted to voters as early as November 1992.

MUNICIPALITY OF METROPOLITAN SEATTLE (METRO TRANSIT)

	1985	1990	2000	*Projected 10-Year Total	Comments
**Rail Ridership	232	149	350 SC 1,750 CR	3,000 SC 1,750 CR	Metro is currently exploring commuter rail service. A preferred alternative will be selected in 1992. Where noted, commuter rail (CR) data estimations have been made. All other figures are for Seattle waterfront streetcar (SC). Commuter rail figures in 10-year total do not show 1991-99 data, as many details are uncertain at this time. Data for Seattle's monorail system, operated by the City of Seattle, have not been provided. ⁰Startup capital
Rail Agency Employees (Include Administrative Support)	2.5	13.9 SC 1 CR	15		
Track Miles	1.6	2.1	2.1 SC 40 CR		
Number of Rail Vehicles (All Types): In Operation	3	4	5 SC 30 CR		
Refurbished	0	1	0	1	
Replaced	0	0	0	0	
**Annual Capital Budget (Rail Only)	$0	$6,544	$0 SC $150,000 CR⁰	$6,544 SC $150,000 CR	
**Annual Operating Budget (Rail Only)	$231	$762	$968 SC $5,500 CR	$7,847 SC $5,500 CR	
**Total Rail Budget	$231	$7,306	$968 SC $155,500 CR	$14,391 SC $155,500 CR	
**Portion of Rail Budget Paid With Federal Funds if Available (Based on Current Law): Capital	$0	$0	$0 SC $25,000 CR	$0 SC $25,000 CR	
Operating	$0	$0	$0	$0	
Total	$0	$0	$0 SC $25,000 CR	$0 SC $25,000 CR	

Governing Board: Council of the Municipality of Metropolitan Seattle
c/o Clerk of the Council MS/93
821 Second Avenue
Seattle, Washington 98104-1598
Telephone: (206) 684-1014   Telefax: (206) 684-1677

Chair: Penelope Peabody

Executive Director: Richard K. Sandaas
Metro MS/94
821 Second Avenue
Seattle, Washington 98104-1598
Telephone: (206) 684-1983   Telefax: (206) 684-1677

Purchasing Agent: Alan Pelton, Equipment Buyer
Metro MS/71
821 Second Avenue
Seattle, Washington 98104-1598
Telephone: (206) 684-1056   Telefax: (206) 684-2168

* Sum of Annual figures for 1991-2000.   ** Ridership and financial figures in thousands.

WASHINGTON, D. C.

Washington Metropolitan Area Transit Authority

The Washington Metropolitan Area Transit Authority (WMATA) operates the second largest rapid rail system in the United States in terms of ridership, with over half a million transit trips for residents and visitors every weekday in Maryland, Virginia and the District of Columbia. The Transit Authority began revenue service in 1976 with five stations and 4.6 miles of track. Today, two-thirds of the system is built and in service at a cost of $7 billion. The current WMATA rail system consists of 664 rail cars, 66 stations, five maintenance yards and 72.7 miles of double-track railroad. An additional 16 miles are under construction, of which 8.3 miles and seven stations will be completed in 1991. The remainder of the 89.5 miles of the adopted regional system will be completed in 1993. In November 1990 the Administration signed a $1.3 billion federal reauthorization bill that will fund approximately ten of the remaining 13 miles of the 103-mile Metrorail system over eight years, beginning in fiscal year 1992.

Ridership remains high. In 1990 the public made more than 145 million Metrorail trips. The highest rail ridership to date occurred on Inauguration Day 1989, with a record 604,000 trips. To provide rail service to the public, the Transit Authority employs 3600 people to operate and maintain the rail system with a current annual operating budget of $265 million. An additional 140 rail cars are on order with delivery scheduled to begin in 1992.

WMATA is an award-winning transit agency. In 1988 the Transit Authority was selected by the American Public Transit Association to receive the Outstanding Achievement Award as the top transit agency in North America.

WASHINGTON METROPOLITAN AREA TRANSIT AUTHORITY (WMATA)

	1985	1990	2000	*Projected 10-Year Total	Comments
**Rail Ridership	100,500	145,000	230,000	1,775,000	
Rail Agency Employees (Include Administrative Support)	3,000	3,600	4200		
Track Miles	60.5	72.7	99.5		Double track. Completed system 103 miles.
Number of Rail Vehicles (All Types): In Operation	528	664	804		
Refurbished	0	0	0	0	
Replaced	0	0	0	0	
**Annual Capital Budget (Rail Only)	$304,969	$201,192	$270,750	$3,481,660	
**Annual Operating Budget (Rail Only)	$165,200	$234,978	$490,000	$3,712,000	
**Total Rail Budget	$470,169	$436,170	$760,750	$7,193,660	
**Portion of Rail Budget Paid With Federal Funds if Available (Based on Current Law): Capital	$249,750	$126,012	$188,405	$2,588,671	
Operating	$0	$0	$0	$0	Federal operating assistance to the region is expended on bus operations.
Total	$249,750	$126,012	$188,405	$2,588,671	

Governing Board: Washington Metropolitan Area Transit Authority Board of Directors
600 Fifth Street, N. W.
Washington D. C., 20001
Telephone: (202) 962-1300   Telefax: (202) 962-1133

Chair: Hilda H. M. Mason
Members: Cleatus E. Barnett, Vice Chair; Joseph Alexander, Second Vice Chair; Gladys W. Mack; Hilda R. Pemberton; Mary Margaret Whipple

General Manager: David L. Gunn
600 Fifth Street, N. W.
Washington D. C., 20001
Telephone: (202) 962-1000   Telefax: (202) 962-1133

Purchasing Agent: Edward T. Rhodes, Director, Office of Procurement
600 Fifth Street, N. W.
Washington D. C., 20001
Telephone: (202) 962-2701   Telefax: (202) 962-2038

Sum of Annual figures for 1991-2000.   ** Ridership and financial figures in thousands.

WVU, Morgantown PRT

The Morgantown People Mover is an automated guideway transit system which provides personal rapid transit (PRT) service between the separated campuses of West Virginia University and the Central Business District.

The system consists of a fleet of electrically powered, rubber-tired, passenger-carrying vehicles, operating on a dedicated guideway network at close headway (vehicle separation). The system provides a safe, comfortable, low polluting, reliable means of transportation. It features year-round operation, as well as direct origin-to-destination service.

Although the Morgantown PRT system is designed to operate in either schedule or demand mode, passenger actions upon entering the system are always the same regardless of the mode in which the system is operating. During those periods when passenger demand is highly predictable, the system is operated on schedule mode. Vehicles are dispatched between origin/destination pairs on a preset schedule. When passenger demand is less predictable, the system is operated in demand mode. Vehicles are then dispatched only in response to a passenger request.

As the first urban deployment of automated guideway transit technology, the objectives of the system are to:

> -Demonstrate the technological, operational and economic
> feasibility of a fully automatic urban transportation system.
> -Determine, through system evaluation and operational
> experience, the potential applicability of personal rapid
> transit to national needs.
> -Provide a functional and economic transportation system for
> the West Virginia University and the City of Morgantown.

	1985	1990	2000	*Projected 10-Year Total	Comments
Rail Ridership	2,450	2,400	2,500	25,000	
Rail Agency Employees (Include Administrative Support)	63	64	60		
Track Miles	8.7	8.7	8.7		Single track
Number of Rail Vehicles (All Types): In Operation	71	71	71		
Refurbished	0	0	0	0	
Replaced	0	0	0	0	
**Annual Capital Budget (Rail Only)	$106	$130	$200	$2,300	
**Annual Operating Budget (Rail Only)	$2,179	$2,536	$3,400	$29,680	
**Total Rail Budget	$2,285	$2,666	$3,600	$31,980	
**Portion of Rail Budget Paid With Federal Funds if Available (Based on Current Law) Capital	$0	$0	$0	$0	65% funded by $45 student fee, remainder funded by the University and DOT research grants.
Operating	$0	$0	$0	$0	Not qualified
Total	$0	$0	$0	$0	

Governing Board: West Virginia University
Transportation & Mail Service
99 Eighth Street
Morgantown, West Virginia 26506
Telephone: (304) 293-5011

Director: Robert J. Bates
West Virginia University — PRT System
99 Eighth Street
Morgantown, West Virginia 26506
Telephone: (304) 293-5011

Purchasing Agent: Thomas Shamberger
West Virginia University — PRT System
99 Eighth Street
Morgantown, West Virginia 26506
Telephone: (304) 293-5011

Montreal Urban Community Transit Corporation

NORTH AMERICAN RAIL TRANSIT

CANADIAN RAIL SYSTEMS

Calgary Transit

Calgary's public transportation system began in 1909 as the Calgary Electric Street Car Railway. Twelve electric streetcars and sixteen miles of track served a rapidly growing pioneer city of 30,000 people. From streetcars to motor buses and electric trolley buses, from gasoline-powered buses to diesel-powered buses, the system has successfully adapted to the fast-paced growth of this Western Canadian city. In 1972, after several name changes, the corporation became known as Calgary Transit and became part of the City of Calgary's Transportation Department.

In the early 1970s Calgary experienced unprecedented growth. Public transportation was urgently required to alleviate the ever-increasing traffic problems created by the growth. Light rail transit was selected for its reliable, proven technology. The LRT Construction Division was formed in September 1977, and the south leg of the LRT opened to the public on May 25, 1981. It was clear from its inception on that the system would greatly change the way citizens of Calgary traveled. The next stage of development included a northeast leg which opened on April 29, 1985. In the central business district a two-kilometer section serves as a transit mall for LRT, buses and emergency vehicles. The next leg of the LRT opened in 1987, connecting the existing south line with service in the city's northwest. On September 3, 1990, a one kilometer extension to the northwest leg was completed. Since the inaugural run a decade ago, Calgary has grown to a population of 693,000 and our C-Train system provides service to 111,290 people daily.

To date about $560 million (Cdn.) has been spent on construction of Calgary's LRT System. Future development will see a 3.5-kilometer extension of the existing south and northwest lines, probably later in this decade, and sometime after the turn of the century construction may start on a new line to the west and underground portion downtown paralleling the transit mall. As the city continues to grow, future LRT right-of-way and station sites are projected. Current projections envision Calgary becoming a city of one million by the year 2010.

	1985	1990	2000	*Projected 10-Year Total	Comments
**Rail Ridership*	15,100	31,200	38,000	345,000	Assumes constant market share.
Rail Agency Employees (Include Administrative Support)	200°	270	300		°Estimation
Track Miles	17.6	18.2	22.3		Double track
Number of Rail Vehicles (All Types): In Operation	52	85[1]	105		[1]83 LRV's and 2 experimental AC cars
Refurbished	0	0	0	0	
Replaced	0	0	0	0	
**Annual Capital Budget* (Rail Only)	$79,361	$25,483	$5,454	$329,548	Financial figures in Canadian dollars
**Annual Operating Budget* (Rail Only)	$12,229	$20,952	$40,793	$288,509	
**Total Rail Budget*	$91,590	$46,435	$46,247	$618,057	
**Portion of Rail Budget Paid With Provincial Funds:*					
Capital	$36,961	$19,112	$4,090	$247,161	
Operating	$991	$4,553	$8,850	$65,690	
Total	$37,952	$23,665	$12,940	$312,851	

Governing Board: City of Calgary Transportation, Transit and Parking Committee
P. O. Box 2100, Station M
Calgary, Alberta
Canada T2P 2M5
Telephone: (403) 268-2430   Telefax: (403) 268-8091

Chair: Alderman R. Magnus
Members: Alderman C. Reid, Vice Chair; Alderman R. Clark; Alderman Y. Fritz; Alderman D. Hodges; Alderman C. Kraychy; Alderman B. Longstaff; Mayor A. Duerr, ex-officio

General Manager: R. H. Irwin
P. O. Box 2100, Station M (#166 S. G.)
Calgary, Alberta
Canada T2P 2M5
Telephone: (403) 277-9800   Telefax: (403) 230-1155

Purchasing Agent: Otto Pipke, Purchasing Manager
Purchasing and Stores Department
P. O. Box 2100, Station M (#8140)
Calgary, Alberta
Canada T2P 2M5
Telephone: (403) 268-5579   Telefax: (403) 268-5523

Sum of Annual figures for 1991-2000.   ** Ridership and financial figures in thousands.

Edmonton Transit

Edmonton, the capital city of the Province of Alberta, Canada, has a public transit system which began in the Fall of 1908, when the Edmonton Radial Railway followed its first route along 21 kilometers of track up Jasper Avenue through the downtown. With a population of 21,000 and a mere four-car fleet, Edmonton remained unique as the first prairie city with a public streetcar system. The first bus route began operating in mid-1932, and the system has since grown to encompass a fleet of over 700 diesel and trolley buses covering 105 routes.

It is supplemented by a light rail system, operating on 11.2 kilometers of track from the northeast area of the city to the heart of downtown. Edmonton was the first city in North America with a population under one million to build a new light rail system. In 1978 the first segment of Route 101 opened with 14 light rail vehicles running on 7.2 kilometers of track at a cost of $64.9 million. The northernmost station, Clareview, opened in 1981. The additional three light rail vehicles and 2.2 kilometers of double track cost $9.2 million. The downtown Bay and Corona Stations began operation in 1983 at a cost of $95.8 million for the .9-kilometer double track and 20 additional LRT vehicles. The most recent station to be completed was Grandin, which began service in September 1989. Construction is continuing on the SLRT segment across the North Saskatchewan River to the University of Alberta, with the first station scheduled for completion in 1992. The LRT offers a virtually pollution-free solution to the problems of traffic congestion and has reduced the need for freeway expansion. It utilizes existing rail right-of-way for four surface stations until it reaches the northeastern boundary of downtown where it enters the tunneled portion for access to five underground station platforms.

Edmonton Transit serves the City of Edmonton, which has a population of 605,538, and is working toward meeting the transportation needs of our customers.

	1985	1990	2000	*Projected 10-Year Total	Comments
. **Rail Ridership	6,998	7,000	17,000	90,000	
. Rail Agency Employees (Include Administrative Support)		100	130		
. Track Miles	6.25	7	11.2		Double track
. Number of Rail Vehicles (All Types): In Operation	34	37	47		Southgate extension
Refurbished	0	0	0	0	
Replaced	0	0	0	0	
. **Annual Capital Budget (Rail Only)	$13,736	$27,000	$28,000	$275,000	All financial figures in Canadian dollars
. **Annual Operating Budget (Rail Only)	$7,449	$9,200	$19,000	$140,000	
. **Total Rail Budget	$21,185	$36,200	$47,000	$415,000	
. **Portion of Rail Budget Paid With Provincial Funds:					
Capital	$10,302	$20,250	$21,000	$206,250	
Operating	$447	$552	$1,140	$8,400	
Total	$10,749	$20,802	$22,140	$214,650	

Governing Board: The Transportation Department is responsible to the City Council of the City of Edmonton.

Mayor Jan Reimer
Richard Picherack, City Manager
5th Floor, Centennial Building
10015 - 103 Avenue
Edmonton, Alberta, Canada T5J 0H1
Telephone: (403) 428-5432   Telefax: (403) 428-3721

General Manager: Gregory Latham, Manager   John Schnablegger
Edmonton Transit   Transportation Department
13th Floor, Century Place   Edmonton Transit
9803 - 102A Avenue
Edmonton, Alberta, Canada T5J 3A3
Telephone: (403) 428-5981   Telefax: (403) 428-5798

Purchasing Agent: Wayne Mandryk, Director Plant and Equipment
Mitchell Garage
11904 - 154 Street
Edmonton Alberta, Canada T5V 1J2
Telephone: (403) 428-4903   Telefax: (403) 428-4752

Sum of Annual figures for 1991-2000.   ** Ridership and financial figures in thousands.

British Columbia Rapid Transit Company LTD. (BC Transit)

SkyTrain is North America's longest completely automated, driverless rapid transit system and forms the backbone of an integrated land-sea-rail transit system serving the Lower Mainland. There are 17 stations along the 24.5-kilometer line running between Waterfront Station in downtown Vancouver and Scott Road Station in Surrey. Gliding along its own right-of-way, SkyTrain moves passengers at speeds up to 80 kilometers per hour, completely independent of the network of crowded roads below. SkyTrain is run by a computerized control system located in the Operations and Maintenance Center in Burnaby, a suburb of Vancouver. In the main control room, a bank of computers and television screens assists operators in monitoring the entire SkyTrain fleet and schedules are adjusted according to fluctuations in demand.

Approximately 100 bus routes connect with SkyTrain stations to form an integrated transit system. Passengers can transfer conveniently from bus to SkyTrain to SeaBus for one fare. SkyTrain is accessible for mobility impaired passengers. Each car has specially designated wheelchair areas and SkyTrain stations are designed so that all services and safety features can be easily located and used. Although initially skeptical, businesses and local governments are now eager to have SkyTrain extended into their municipalities. They see it as a catalyst for positive change. Current and planned developments along the Vancouver-Burnaby-New Westminster-Surrey corridor amount to $7 billion in direct spending with $21 billion in spin-offs.

In July 1989 the Honorable Rita M. Johnston, minister responsible for transit, announced the expansion of SkyTrain service. As part of the provincial government's billion dollar commitment to public transit, the first phase of SkyTrain service to Coquitlam will arrive at Lougheed Mall in 1995. The SkyTrain guideway will be extended 4.3 kilometers in Surrey, from the Scott Road Station to Whalley. Two of the three new SkyTrain stations being constructed on the Whalley extension are financed entirely by the private sector, with the third financed by the private sector, local government and BC Transit. The SkyTrain extension to Whalley is estimated to cost $127 million and the new line is scheduled to be in revenue service by the end of 1993.

BRITISH COLUMBIA RAPID TRANSIT COMPANY LTD. (BC TRANSIT)

	1985°	1990	2000	*Projected 10-Year Total	Comments
Rail Ridership	—	33,500	60,000	423,400	°SkyTrain did not begin revenue service until 1986.
Rail Agency Employees (Include Administrative Support)	—	313	422		
Track Miles	—	14.9	31.8		Double track
Number of Rail Vehicles (All Types): In Operation	—	114	250		
Refurbished	—	0	0	0	
Replaced	—	0	0	0	
**Annual Capital Budget (Rail Only)	—	$25,800	$215,450	$1,221,500	Includes route expansion to Whalley for FY 1990
**Annual Operating Budget (Rail Only)	—	$29,745	$72,340	$477,840	Financial figures in Canadian dollars.
**Total Rail Budget	—	$55,545	$287,790	$1,699,340	
**Portion of Rail Budget Paid With Provincial Funds:					
Capital	—	$0	$161,588	$916,125	
Operating	—	$0	$36,170	$238,920	
Total	—	$0	$197,758	$1,155,045	

Governing Board: **Province of British Columbia**
Minister responsible for transit

General Manager: Larry Ward
6800 14th Avenue
Vancouver, British Columbia
Canada V3N 4S7
Telephone: (604) 520-3641   Telefax: (604) 521-2818

Purchasing Agent: Larry Kesslar, Materials Manager
6800 14th Avenue
Vancouver, British Columbia
Canada V3N 4S7
Telephone: (604) 520-3641   Telefax: (604) 521-2818

Sum of Annual figures for 1991-2000.   ** Ridership and financial figures in thousands.

Government of Ontario Transit (GO Transit)

GO Transit is the Province of Ontario's interregional passenger transportation system for the greater Metropolitan Toronto region, serving a population of four million in an area of more than 8,000 square kilometers (3,000 square miles).

GO, which stands for Government of Ontario, began as a three-year experiment in May 1967 with a single rail line along Lake Ontario. It has since succeeded and expanded beyond all expectations.

GO Train service has grown into a seven-corridor network, connecting with GO buses, local transit, and the extensive Toronto Transit Commission system (TTC). GO Bus service started in September 1970 as an extension of the original Lakeshore train but is now a full-fledged network in its own right, both augmenting train service and serving communities not reached by rail, as far away as 90 kilometers (55 miles) from downtown Toronto; the seven-corridor bus network also connects with the TTC and other municipal transit systems at many points.

Lakeshore GO Trains carried 2 1/2 million passengers the first year. Today the combined rail and bus system carries 34 1/2 million annually.

GO runs 154 trains and 1,200 bus trips daily, transporting 131,000 passengers on an average weekday — 94,000 on trains and 37,000 by bus. Ninety-five percent of the train ridership is to and from Union Station in downtown Toronto, while 69% of all bus passengers travel to and from Metropolitan Toronto.

GOVERNMENT OF ONTARIO TRANSIT (GO TRANSIT)

	1985	1990	2000	*Projected 10-Year Total	Comments
Rail Ridership	15,284	24,820	44,500	350,000	Figures include operating contracts with CN and CP
Rail Agency Employees (Include Administrative Support)		550	N/A		CN & CP employees
Track Miles	212	268	296		Only 9 miles owned
Number of Rail Vehicles (All Types): In Operation	197	351	488		Includes bi-level coaches and locomotives
Refurbished		12	0	240	
Replaced		14	0	14	
**Annual Capital Budget (Rail Only)		$266,473	$115,746	$2,468,048	1985 financial figures not separately available for rail
**Annual Operating Budget (Rail Only)		$73,569	N/A	N/A	
**Total Rail Budget		$340,042	$115,746	$2,468,048	All financial figures in Canadian dollars
**Portion of Rail Budget Paid With Provincial Funds:					0Total capital budget for all purposes, including rail
Capital	$25,350[0]	$266,473	$115,746	$2,468,048	
Operating	$46,973	$25,747			Provincial agency 65% farebox recovery 35% Provincial subsidy
Total	$72,323	$292,220	$115,746	$2,468,048	

Governing Board: **Government Of Ontario Transit Board of Directors**

Chair: L. H. Parsons
1120 Finch Avenue West
Toronto, Ontario , Canada M3J 3J8
Telephone: (416) 665-9211   Telefax: (416) 665-9006

Members: G. W. Herrema, Vice Chair; R. F. Bean; E. R. King; P. D. Pomeroy; A. Tonks; R. J. Wynott

General Manager: Tom Smith
1120 Finch Avenue West
Toronto, Ontario, Canada M3J 3J8
Telephone: (416) 665-9211   Telefax: (416) 665-9006

Purchasing Agent: Ingo Sass, Manager
Materials Management
1120 Finch Avenue West
Toronto, Ontario, Canada M3J 3J8
Telephone: (416) 665-9211   Telefax: (416) 665-9006

Sum of Annual figures for 1991-2000.   ** Ridership and financial figures in thousands.

Toronto Transit Commission

The Toronto Transit Commission (TTC) was established in 1954 under the jurisdiction of the Municipality of Metropolitan Toronto. Its mandate is to oversee a comprehensive public transportation operation for the City of Toronto and surrounding municipalities that make up Metropolitan Toronto.

On March 30, 1954, the TTC opened the 7.4-kilometer Yonge subway line, the first subway line built in North America after World War II. Nine years later, the University subway line was opened, followed by the opening of the Bloor-Danforth line in 1967. Today, the subway and rapid transit system is about 60 kilometers with 65 stations.

On June 22, 1990, the TTC officially opened the Harbourfront Light Rail Transit Line, the first streetcar line to be built in Toronto in more than 60 years. The $59.3 million line, built on its own dedicated right-of-way, stretches more than two kilometers, from Union Station along Queens Quay to the Spadina Loop.

In 1990 the TTC carried 183 million passengers on its subway and rapid transit line and a total of 459 million passengers on all its modes of transportation.

In April 1990 the Province of Ontario announced its commitment to spend $4.32 billion over the next ten years on public transit expansion including extending the Bloor-Danforth subway line, connecting the Yonge and Spadina subway lines, extending the Scarborough Rapid Transit line, building the Sheppard subway line and the Mississauga busway, and extending the Harbourfront Light Rail Transit Line. Initial planning has begun and the projects are scheduled to be completed within ten years.

The Toronto Transit Commission is North America's second largest public transit authority, carrying 1.5 million passengers each day. It employs 10,500 staff and operates more than 2,800 surface and subway vehicles in Metropolitan Toronto.

	1985	1990	2000	*Projected 10-Year Total	Comments
**Rail Ridership	270.4 HR 104.6 LR 5.1 ICTS	294.9 HR 80.9 LR 9.1 ICTS	N/A	N/A	HR = Heavy rail LR = Light rail ICTS = Intermediate Capacity Transit System (Scarborough)
Rail Agency Employees (Include Administrative Support)	9,025 R 190 T	10,472 R 125 T 49 PT	12,100 R 150 T 100 PT		
Track Miles⁰	33.80 HR 45.59 LR 4.05 ICTS	33.80 HR 47.19 LR 3.98 ICTS	N/A		R = Regular T = Temporary PT = Part-time
Number of Rail Vehicles (All Types): In Operation	630 HR 284 LR 24 ICTS	622 HR 270 LR 28 ICTS	N/A		⁰Route miles
Refurbished	—	—	—	—	
Replaced	—	—	—	—	Projected 10-year forecast includes estimates to reflect the "Let's Move" Transit Initiatives announced by the Ontario Government as part of the Province of Ontario's $5 Billion Rapid Transit Agenda for the 90's.
**Annual Capital Budget (Rail Only)	$157,221	$76,504	$192,400	$8,521,400	
**Annual Operating Budget (Rail Only)	$192,797	$285,728	N/A	N/A	
**Total Rail Budget	$350,018	$362,232	N/A	N/A	All financial figures in Canadian dollars
**Portion of Rail Budget Paid With Provincial Funds:					
Capital	$117,915	$57,378	$144,300	$6,391,050	75% Provincial share
Operating	$29,997	$43,532	N/A	N/A	Normally 68% comes from fares; remainder is split between Province and Metro Toronto
Total	$147,912	$100,710	N/A	N/A	

Governing Board: **Toronto Metro Council**
390 Bay Street
Toronto, Ontario
Canada M5H 3Y7
Telephone: (416) 392-4051   Telefax: (416) 392-4120

Chair: Lois Griffin
Members: Michael Colle, Vice Chair; Commissioner Alan Tonks; Commissioner Bev Salmon; Commissioner Brian Harrison

Chief General Manager: Al Leach
1900 Yonge Street
Toronto, Ontario
Canada M4S 1Z2
Telephone: (416) 393-4000   Telefax: (416) 485-9394

Purchasing Agent: Executive Office of Toronto Transit Commission
1900 Yonge Street
Toronto, Ontario
Canada M4S 1Z2
Telephone: (416) 393-4000   Telefax: (416) 485-9394

* Sum of Annual figures for 1991-2000.   ** Ridership and financial figures in thousands.

Montreal Urban Community Transit

Montreal Urban Community Transit (MUCT) is a public corporation responsible for public transit activities in the Montreal Urban Community territory. The Board of Director consists of elected representatives from the Urban Community, the City of Montreal, the suburbs' municipalities and patron representatives.

The original subway network, with 28 stations spanning 25.9 kilometers, was designed, built and financed entirely by the City of Montreal. Design work began in 1962 and within five years the subway began revenue service. Extensions were added gradually, bringing the number of stations to 65 and the revenue network to 64 kilometers. Annual subway ridership is 200,000,000. The subway is connected to more than 30 commercial buildings. Two underground corridors link subway stations and commercial facilities in the downtown area. Feasibility studies are currently underway to evaluate extensions of existing lines and construction of a new line.

MUCT was involved in the commuter train business in 1982 when two service contracts were signed with Canadian National and Canadian Pacific. The purpose was to integrate the local commuter train network to the surface and subway MUCT network. One line runs from Central Station in downtown Montreal to Deux-Montagnes terminus a few kilometers outside Montreal Urban Community. The other line runs from Windsor Station to Rigaud, a town approximately 64 kilometers from downtown Montreal. Fare structure in the Montreal Urban Community territory allows free tranfers between commuter trains, buses and the subway network.

In 1984 the Windsor Station to Rigaud line was upgraded to increase ridership. Annual ridership grew from 1.8 millions passengers in 1983 to 3.6 million in 1990. Major renovation on the Central Station — Deux-Montagnes line is planned over the next two or three years. The annual ridership in 1983 was 3.6 million passengers. In 1990 the annual ridership was 4.7 million passengers.

	1985	1990	2000	*Projected 10-Year Total	Comments
1. **Rail Ridership	200,600	216,428	252,557	2,271,535	
2. Rail Agency Employees (Include Administrative Support)	2260°	2407	2200		° Estimate
3. Track Miles	56.9 CR 31.4 Subway	56.9 CR 38.1 Subway	59.9 CR 48.7 Subway		CR=Commuter Rail Double Track
4. Number of Rail Vehicles (All Types): In Operation	893	923	1005		
Refurbished	0	55	759	814	
Replaced	0	0	124	124	
5. **Annual Capital Budget (Rail Only)	0	$5,600	$46,000	$550,000	All financial figures in Canadian dollars.
6. **Annual Operating Budget (Rail Only)	$221,600	$301,000	$426,000	$3,895,000	Inflation rate of 4.5%
7. **Total Rail Budget	$221,600	$306,600	$472,000	$4,445,000	
8. **Portion of Rail Budget Paid With Provincial Funds:					
Capital	$143,600	$186,700	$12,000	$234,000	
Operating	N/A	$5,600	$20,000	$50,000	
Total	$143,600	$192,300	$32,000	$284,000	Subsidy projections include commuter rail only.

Governing Board: Montreal Urban Community Transit
360, St-Jacques ouest
Bureau 701
Montreal, Quebec
Canada H2Y 1P5
Telephone: (514) 280-5531

President: Robert Perreault
Members: Michel Hamelin, Malcolm C. Knox, Ginette L'Heureux, Yvon Labrosse, Abe Limonchik, Yvon Marsolais, Sybil Murray-Denis, Raymond Savard

President/ General Director: Louise Roy
159, St-Antoine ouest
10th Floor
Montreal, Quebec
Canada H2Z 1H3
Telephone: (514) 280-5150   Telefax: (514) 280-5193

Purchasing Agent: Jacques Durocher
8845, Boulevard St-Laurent
5th Floor
Montreal, Quebec
Canada H2N 1M2
Telephone: (514) 280-4900   Telefax: (514) 280-4933

133

* Sum of Annual figures for 1991-2000.   ** Ridership and financial figures in thousands.

August 1, 1991

AMERICAN PUBLIC TRANSIT ASSOCIATION
ROD DIRIDON, VICE PRESIDENT–RAIL TRANSIT

MODAL COMMITTEES

Rail Safety Review Board
Chairman, Robert G. Schwab
General Manager
Port Authority Transit Corporation

Commuter Rail Committee
Chairman, Michael J. Nielsen
Senior Director, Corporate Administration
Metra

Heavy Rail Committee
Chairman, Chester E. Colby
Director
Metro-Dade Transit Agency

Light Rail Committee
Chairman, Hal Wanaselja
Project Manager
Bechtel Civil Company

A.G.T. Committee
Chairman, George A. Swede
Transportation Development Specialist
Los Angeles County Transportation Commission

Inter-City Ground Transportation Systems Committee
Chairman, Joseph S. Silien
Director, Business Planning and Development
ABB Traction, Inc.

Multi-Modal Operations Planning Committee
Chairman, Howard P. Benn
Asst. V.P.-Operations Planning
New York City Transit Authority

STAFF ADVISORS

FRANK J. CIHAK, Chief Engineer & Deputy Executive Vice President–Technical Services

EDWARD M. GREGERMAN, Director-Rail Technology–Technical Services

RAIL TRANSIT STEERING COMMITTEE

CHAIRMAN, Ronald J. Hartman
General Manager/Administrator
Mass Transit Administration of Maryland
VICE CHAIRMAN, Richard R. Kelly
Vice President/General Manager
Port Authority Trans-Hudson Corporation

TECHNICAL COMMITTEES

Power, Signals & Communications Committee
Chairman, George S. Pristach
President
Trelcon, Inc.

- Wire & Cable
- Power
- Signals
- Communications

Rail Safety Committee
Chairman, Lawrence M. Engleman
Director of Safety
Mass Transit Administration of Maryland

- Industrial Safety
- System Safety Program Management
- Emergency Preparedness/ Life Safety

Way & Structures Committee
Chairman, Vincent P. Mahon
Dept. Mgr., Power & Way
San Francisco Bay Area Rapid Transit District

- Equipment
- Structures
- Track
- Yards & Shops
- Elevators & Escalators

Rolling Stock Equipment Committee
Chairman, W. Erich Vogel
Chief Officer,
Integrated Logistics Support
Southeastern Pennsylvania Transportation Authority

- Commuter Rail
- Heavy Rail
- Light Rail
- Inter-City Rail
- A.G.T.

Construction Committee
Chairman, Richard K. Sandaas
Executive Director
Municipality of Metropolitan Seattle

- Construction Engineering
- Construction Management
- Construction Support
- Pre-Construction

Rail Operations Committee
Chairman, William E. Callier
Dir., Rail Transportation
Metropolitan Atlanta Rapid Transit Authority

- Operations Control Centers
- Transit Operations Management
- Railroad Operations Management

Research & Development Committee
Chairman, Ronald T. Yutko
Director of Engineering
Metro-North Commuter Railroad Company

- Computer Applications
- Systems & Subsystems
- Materials Procurement
- R.A.M.D.
- Standards & Specifications
- Operations & Maintenance

Index